# Farewell to Spandau

# Farewell to Spandau

Tony Le Tissier

First published in the United Kingdom in 1994 by
Ashford, Buchan & Enright, Leatherhead, Surrey

Second edition published in 2008 by
The History Press
Cirencester Road · Chalford · Stroud · Gloucestershire · GL6 8PE

British Library Cataloguing in Publication Data
A catalogue record for this book is available from the British Library.

ISBN  978 0 7509 4837 1

Typesetting and origination by
The History Press Limited.
Printed and bound in England by
Ashford Colour Press Ltd, Gosport, Hants

# Contents

*To my wife and children
and all those friends and colleagues
who have made life in Berlin
so full and so interesting
over the years*

# List of Plates

1. Barrack block used by Allied guards during their duty months.

2. The Main Gate used by the Soviet guards for their accommodation

3. Aerial view of Prison taken shortly after Hess's death with the new perimeter fence and gate installed. The ruins of the old prison laundry with its chimney can be seen on the left with the disused workshops behind. Hess's lift is hidden by the trees left of the main cell block. The ruins of the prison hospital can be seen bottom right and part of Brooke Barracks top right.

4. Watching a Parade
Lt Col Savin, Tony Le Tissier, the Adjutant of the 2nd Bn The Royal Irish Rangers, Lt Col Durofeyev, Michel Planet and Darold Keane on the 1st July, 1984.

5. Michel Planet Gendarmerie Lt Col, Captain Francis Hobbs (ADC to GOC), Tony Le Tissier, Lt Col Chernykh, Lt Col Rory Forsyth and some officers and a warrant officer of the 1st Bn The Prince of Wales's Own Regiment of Yorkshire on 1 February, 1983.

East–West relations
6. & 7. Tony Le Tissier sharing a joke with Yuri Prontchev and a colleague from the Soviet Embassy.

8. Adjourning to the Mess after a Parade.

9. The Main Building seen from the top of the Mess. The Administration Block with the chapel above, the Tower over the cruciform centre of the Cell Block and a dormitory wing. Tower No.6 and the ruins of the prison hospital are in front.

10. The Governors' Mess, No.21 Wilhelmstrasse.

11. Hess in the second position on the cabinet bench at a session of the Reichstag held in the Kroll Opera, enraptured by his Führer. (ATB)

In the Mess
12. Lt Col Savin with Valentina.
13. Major Yuri Pliev, Tony Le Tissier and Lt Col Gennady Savin.

14. Tower No.3 seen from the prisoner's exercise path with evidence of the previous Allied prisoners' work showing under the trees on the right.

15. The guards' track leading into the broader prisoner's path in the north-western corner of the garden with the Portakabin beyond.

16. Christmas in the Governors' Mess 1985, with Michel Planet, 'Katya', Tony Le Tissier, Lt Col Chernykh flanked by two BRIXMIS interpreters, Darold Keane and Senior Lieutenant Dmitri Naumenko.

28. & 29. The prison site completely cleared except for trees.

30. The temporary mess in No.24 where the run-down of the prison administration was completed after the Royal Engineers had surrounded the building with Dannert wire on Soviet request. Nos. 25, 25A and Smuts Barracks in the background. The low wall on the right once carried an electrified fence.

31. Aerial view of the Britannia Centre in 1991. The two trees growing out of the patio are the horse chestnuts of the old prison courtyard. The clusters of trees to the rear are relics of Hess's garden. (ATB)

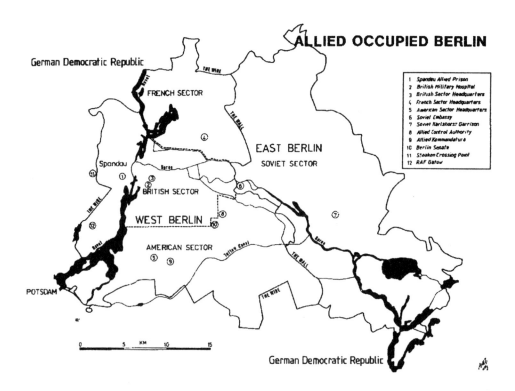

# SPANDAU ALLIED PRISON

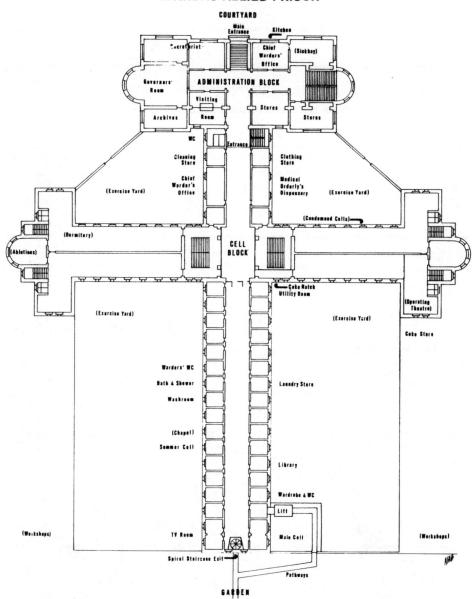

Guard Changing – 1st Bn The Royal Highland Fusiliers handing over to a Gendarmie Nationale guard on the 1st February 1987.

# Preface

The mischievous propagation of certain myths in connection with the fate of Rudolf Hess has prompted me to try to put the record straight with an account of my own experiences in Berlin as the last British Governor of Spandau Allied Prison.

I must emphasise that this is a very personal view of the subject, and that the opinions and attitudes expressed are entirely my own and should not be taken as expressions of official government policy.

The atmosphere in which the events in this book occurred has vanished for ever with the winds of change that blew away the Cold War. The prison site gave way to 'The Britannia Centre,' a shopping and social services precinct for the British garrison, whose days were numbered, but the peripheral buildings have been beautifully restored as part of the same complex.

I would like to express my gratitude to Mr Bernard Levin of *The Times* and Miss Catherine Field of the *Observer* for their most kind permission to reproduce extracts from certain articles, and to the Special Investigation Branch (Royal Military Police), the Ullstein Bildesdienst, and *After the Battle* magazine for permission to reproduce some of their photographs.

To avoid unnecessary embarrassment, I have deliberately omitted those names of people not publicly disclosed during the course of events related here.

*AHLeT*
*Berlin, 1994*

# I

# Spandau Allied Prison

On 17 August 1987, Allied Prisoner No. 7, Rudolf Hess, died at the age of ninety-three. This 'profoundly evil man, justly convicted and condemned . . . at Nuremberg,' had taken his own life, confounding all the quadripartite contingency plans covering his demise. He had been in captivity for over forty-eight years, ever since his spectacular flight to Scotland in May 1941, the last twenty years as the only inmate of Spandau Allied Prison.

For the last few years of his life I was the British representative on the Board of Governors of Spandau Allied Prison. As such I was responsible to the British government for the custody and welfare of this extraordinary character, whose career, actions and fate have aroused so much worldwide curiosity and speculation over the years.

I was serving as a lieutenant-colonel in the then Corps of Royal Military Police (RMP) when I came to Berlin in January 1976 to take up the appointment of Assistant Provost-Marshal (APM) at the British Sector Headquarters. As APM – the confusing use of the prefix 'Assistant' for lieutenant-colonels' staff appointments was later dropped and the RMP organisation in Berlin changed – I was responsible to the British Commandant (the Major-General in charge of the British Sector) for both 247 (Berlin) Provost Company and its Helmstedt Detachment, which had been my first command as a major back in 1968–70. This role also entailed responsibility for officially sponsored British traffic on the autobahn corridor connecting Berlin with the Federal Republic (West Germany), liaison with the Soviet traffic control organisations at either end of the corridor and also with the guard detachment at the Soviet War Memorial in the Tiergarten, as well as dealing with incidents involving the East German authorities on the British Sector boundaries.

Unfortunately, the role of APM had diminished in interest since 1970 as the consolidation of the Wall and the wire fencing around the Western Sectors of Berlin reduced the number of border incidents that had previously added zest to the responsibilities involved. Then, in 1977, at a time when the British Army was terribly badly paid, with my financial resources exhausted, three children at boarding schools, and my car in urgent need of replacement, I received the offer of a post of equivalent rank with the Public Safely Branch of the British Military Government (BMG). Acceptance made me financially viable once more and gave me the chance of continuing to live and serve in a city that fascinated me, and still does.

Of course, 'Murphy's Law' applied, and a few months later armed services pay and pensions were dramatically increased. However, the prospects of continuing staff duties within the then strictly limited sphere of the RMP, whatever the promotion prospects, held no attractions for me, so I had no regrets on that score. Also my 'civilianisation' involved no dramatic severance from the more pleasant aspects of Army life, as I was to continue in close daily contact, making and retaining even more friends among the military as I stayed and others came and went over the years.

At this point I should explain the basic structure of government in Berlin under Allied occupation, which was not only unique but also somewhat complicated.

The supreme authorities were the ambassadors of the four victorious powers, these being the British, French and American

Ambassadors to the German Federal Republic and the Soviet Ambassador to the German Democratic Republic (East Germany). This was a residual capacity from the old, post-war, Allied Control Authority (ACA) days, when Germany was governed from the ACA building in Heinrich von Kleist Park (where in my time the quadripartite Berlin Air Safety Centre [BASC] continued to operate, and would do so until the reunification of Germany).

In 1948 the Soviets walked out of both the ACA and the Allied Kommandatura, the latter establishment being responsible for Greater Berlin, vainly hoping that the system would collapse. This failed to occur, so next in line of seniority in the Western Sectors came the British, French and American Commandants (of major-general rank), each of whom had a Minister as his Deputy Commandant and supporting staff provided by their respective foreign offices to assist and advise them in the governing role. Also directly under the individual Commandants were the military headquarters necessary for maintaining their respective garrisons. By these means, and working within the spirit of the Quadripartite Agreement of 1971 (QA), despite differences of interpretation of its meaning with the Soviets, the Western Allies persistently continued to maintain those basic rights in Berlin which enabled the democratically elected city government at Schönberg Town Hall to function under the Governing Mayor.

Soviet political interests in the Western Sectors were covered from the Embassy on the Unter den Linden, and commercial and consular interests by a Consulate-General introduced under the terms of the QA and located in the American Sector of the city. Both these establishments naturally provided bases for the ubiquitous KGB, the Soviet espionage service.

However, the British Military Government, *le Gouvernement Militaire Français de Berlin* and the US Mission, each continued to field members of the various controlling Committees of the Allied Kommandatura in the political, economic, legal and public safety areas, to cover their residual roles in the administration of the city.

My work as Number Two in the Public Safely Branch brought me into close contact with the Berlin Police, as well as my French and American colleagues, and gave me a greater insight into the complex workings of the city, all of which was to prove very useful in my next appointment. Like many others before me, I was fascinated by the genuine spirit of co-operation and commitment to the well-being of the city that existed at all levels among the Western Allies.

This was particularly true of the British Headquarters, where the Commandant's thrice-weekly 'morning prayers,' attended by all the senior staff officers and departmental heads of the British Military Government and Sector Headquarters, enabled an open exchange of information and co-ordination of effort in the common cause.

Both as APM and in Public Safety, I had some limited contact with Spandau Allied Prison in rehearsing and conducting convoys for the escorting of an ambulance conveying Hess between the prison and the British Military Hospital (BMH). These convoys were intended to deter any attempt to rescue him from captivity, very much as was described in Daniel Carney's *The Square Circle* and later depicted in the film *Wild Geese 2*. Although the route we used did not provide such ready facilities for a rescue attempt as the film suggested, the distance travelled being barely two miles and that mainly on the broad, open expanse of the Heerstrasse, the filming locations used drew my admiration or ingenuity in portraying the story of the book. As a coincidence, I was leaving the famous Pariser Bar restaurant in Kantstrasse in the early hours one morning, when a convoy of ambulances and staff cars, driven by what looked like Royal Military Policemen and escorted by Berlin Police, drove past. For a moment I thought there must have been a hideous accident involving British personnel in East Berlin. In fact these were actors on their way to film the switch scene in the Budapester Strasse tunnel.

Then in 1981, as an economic measure, it was decided to localise the appointment of joint Prison-Governor-cum-Allied-Liaison-

and-Protocol-Officer-cum-British-Resident, which had for some time been occupied by a series of FCO Grade 6 officers, usually ex-Consul-Generals, on their last appointments before retirement. In effect the Treasury transferred the cost of the incumbent's salary to the Occupation Budget financed by the German Federal Government.

The Allied liaison and protocol aspect was a residual role, like that of the ambassadors, these officers too having been originally based on the ACA building. Their role involved the accreditation of diplomats to the British Sector of Berlin, national representation at official functions in diplomatic circles, and low-key exchange of protests and so on, with the equivalent-ranking Protocol Officer at the Soviet Embassy on the Unter den Linden in East Berlin. It also involved the preparation of guest lists for the annual Queen's Birthday Parade on the Maifeld; the seating plans for it, allowing for all the complications of precedence that protocol in this city entailed; the guest lists for the reception at the Headquarters afterwards; and, every second year, the protocol arrangements for the British Berlin Tattoo in the Deutschlandhalle.

The British Resident aspect was another residual role from the early days, when the Resident had been the key man linking the destitute local authorities with the military government. It still involved liaison with the mayors of all four districts in the British Sector, but otherwise had diminished to the issue of game licences to the few in the British community requiring them.

I was offered this post – British Governor of Spandau Prison (plus all the rest of it) – under local contract with equivalent to UK-based status, and eventually started in my new office on 1 October 1981. From then on my working life was to be far more complicated than ever before, if also utterly fascinating and often highly enjoyable.

My retiring predecessor introduced me to the prison by taking me along to his final Governor's meeting at the prison on Thursday, 25 September 1981. Charles was a loner, a very private person with a poker face and a wicked sense of humour. He spoke laconically, and it was often difficult to tell whether he was being serious or simply pulling your leg. I liked him, but I knew he was not an easy person to work with, mainly because others lacked his pithy wit and, failing to match him, misunderstood his manner. It was only on that morning that I discovered that he had arranged with BMG to stay on for a while on contract as a warder, a decision that led to some upset and misgivings among his contemporaries, but in fact was eventually to work out quite well.

Together we were driven from the British Sector Headquarters in a BMG staff car and dropped off in front of the prison's forbidding entrance. We were standing on a short cobbled driveway at right-angles to Spandau's Wilhelmstrasse. A plate on the side of the gatehouse door marked the building as No. 23. The old prison perimeter walls extended either side with a more modern watchtower capping the far corners, from each of which an armed British soldier eyed us curiously. Outside the walls a tall wire fence boxed in a narrow grassy area through which ran the concrete foundations of the electrified fence that had once been there. Outside the existing fence a parallel drive connected some three-storey buildings either side with their gardens, Nos. 21 and 22 to the right and Nos. 24, 25 and 25A to the left. Beyond No. 25A lay Smuts Barracks, containing the garrison's armoured, engineering, and educational elements.

We rang the bell beside the metal-covered wooden Main Gate and were admitted by a warder through a wicket inset on one side. I found myself within the high-ceilinged passage of the gatehouse leading to a cobbled yard beyond. A British sentry with his back to the light held his rifle aimed above our heads while the postern was open, then slammed into a 'Present Arms', the sounds echoing between the flagstones and the beamed ceiling above. Charles explained that the Governors were entitled to such a salute, something neither of us had been senior enough to experience during our military service. He then led me into the gatehouse, where I had to sign in against a provisional pass previously signed by all four Governors.

We went out again into the archway past the rigid sentry and on into the cobbled yard, where two large horse chestnut trees, one on either side, were already dropping their conkers. The grim façade of the Administration Block rose before us, its windows barred to the second floor, above which the dirty windows of the chapel rose a further two stories, the sills heaped and stained with pigeon droppings.

We pushed open a heavy, barred-and-windowed double door and went up a flight of stone steps to a further set of doors at the top. A polished stone floor led forwards under a vaulted ceiling to where a painted metal wall cut across the broad passageway, beyond which lay the Cell Block. We turned right into a short corridor with wooden doors on either side and a larger door across the end.

Charles opened the door on the right and led me into the Secretariat, two small, cluttered offices furnished with old-fashioned cupboards and desks. I was introduced to two elderly gentlemen, one of Yugoslav and the other of Belgian extraction, who were the prison's long-serving secretaries, both then long overdue for retirement.

From the second office we turned left into the Governors' Room, a large room with a vaulted ceiling lit by a window bay forming the northern end of the Administrative Block. Immediately before the door was a long green-topped conference table lined by cane-back wooden chairs. In the centre on the left were double doors leading to the corridor, which were backed by the wide single door that I had seen from the other side. In the left far corner was a small old-fashioned safe on a stand and next to it a metal door leading to the Archives. Between the conference table and the bay windows was a battery of four identical, modern desks. On the far wall hung a large map of Berlin and the only picture in the room, showing Soviet troops marching out through the prison gate and American troops marching in, which on close inspection turned out to be two photographs joined together to make the action look simultaneous.

I was introduced to the people sitting around the table. At the near end sat Lieutenant-Colonel Savin, the Soviet Governor, wearing Artillery insignia on the black facings of his khaki uniform, and next to him his interpreter, Senior Lieutenant Roshkov, wearing Infantry insignia on red facings. On the left, with his back to the double doors, sat the French Governor, Michel Planet, and opposite him Darold W. Keane, the American Governor, sitting beside the BMG interpreter. Charles sat down in a modern swivel chair that looked quite incongruous in these surroundings and invited me to sit alongside him.

One aspect of the Soviet walk-out from the Allied Kommandatura was that the sequence of the monthly rotation of chairmanship among the Four Powers, commencing each January, subsequently operated on two different cycles, the tripartite one for the Western Sectors being British-American-French, the quadripartite one, by which the prison continued to operate, following the sequence British-French-Soviet-American. September being a British month, Charles called the meeting to order and set about business, which mainly concerned the administration of the prison with items such as replacement of staff, the prisoner's requests, approval of passes for visitors, coke deliveries, and so on. A strict sequence was followed round the table on every point, calling first on the French, then the Soviet and lastly the American Governors. The vaulted ceiling presented considerable acoustic problems, and it was soon obvious to me that the Chairman had to be careful to ensure that translations were complete before the next person spoke, as whenever two persons spoke simultaneously all distinction was lost. Fortunately the French had long since agreed to work in English at these meetings, thereby saving much time as well as the need for another interpreter.

Once the meeting was over, Charles took me to meet the prisoner. We went back to the steel door in the hallway, where he pressed a bell. A warder in plain grey uniform and bearing a bunch of enormous keys opened the door and let us into the Cell Block. The broad passageway continued a few yards and then opened out even wider at a point under the main tower forming the crux of the building.

In a corner stood a curious kind of stretcher designed to carry a patient in a seated position. A set of steel doors, one of them open, led through to the Cell Block proper beyond. We walked along a non-slip mat laid on the highly polished stone floor, passing rows of cell doors painted a light brown against the dark cream of the walls. At regular intervals, brackets supported the walkways above, which were otherwise hidden by a white-painted metal ceiling. At the end of the block a curious half-octagonal structure covered the spiral staircase leading down into the garden, and windows high in the wall on either side admitted some daylight. There was a small table and an armchair in the passage for the use of the attendant warder, at that time absent for lunch.

Charles knocked on the penultimate door on the left. '*Herein!*' We went into the first of what had obviously once been two cells. Hess was eating his lunch, sitting up on a hospital bed that almost filled the end cell. The bed was canted to keep his feet higher than his bottom and to support his back. It was flanked by two small tables on which were arranged several covered dishes of food and a collection of spectacles and alarm clocks. Stuck to the wall behind the bed were two maps depicting either side of the moon's surface. In the near cell were two small tables covered in books and newspapers, and a small record-player.

Hess made as if to get up but Charles signalled him to stay where he was. Hess put his dish and spoon to one side and looked at me curiously from under his deep brows. Charles then introduced me and said I would be taking over from him at the end of the month. Hess nodded amicably, and expressed surprise when Charles announced that he would be staying on as a warder. We then left him to get on with his lunch.

Charles explained that Hess ordered his meals by means of a modern child's slate, on which he wrote his menu with a stick. Once the meal had been prepared the 'slate' was returned clear of his impressions. (In fact he had several of these slates for communication with his kitchen, and with the Secretariat for his everyday requirements of paper handkerchiefs and so on, whereas formal requests to the Governors, *Gesuche*, had to be made in writing on sheets of paper such as those issued to him for his weekly letter.) Two cooks were employed solely to cater for him. He was pernickety about his diet, which was mainly vegetarian and contained no salt.

Charles then showed me round the prisoner's exercise area. We went down the very narrow spiral staircase to the garden. The prison cellars were only sunk about a metre below ground level, so access to the garden was by means of a glass-panelled door one full spiral down the stairs, halfway to the cellar. Just inside this door was an old telephone, connected to the gatehouse, for emergency use. From the door a concrete path with a railing led down to a dirt path running parallel to the outer wall along the centre of the garden for its entire length. This path also formed part of the guards' perimeter track within the walls, and both ends of the garden now lacked the gates that had originally sealed it off. The only obtrusion was Tower No. 3, overlooking the garden halfway along the rear perimeter wall but almost completely obscured by the trees.

This area always struck me as a delightful haven of peace in Berlin. First, there was a variety of trees and bushes, seemingly unkempt but in fact pruned annually, some of them having forced their way through the traces of the garden patches made and tended by the other six Nuremberg prisoners so many years before. There were plenty of wild flowers, and even the remains of a trellis with wild roses still growing around it. I could readily accept Charles's comment that Hess rarely missed the opportunity to exercise here morning and afternoon.

Then there was the Portakabin, a metal container-like object, which had a window and door on the nearside, the far side being glass and having sliding glass doors. Here Hess could sit to read his newspapers with his feet up on a second chair, cushioned and wrapped in blankets in inclement weather, and with electric heaters and standard lamps to warm and light him if necessary. Here he could take a nap, or sit outside in summer when he so wished. There was also a small park-type bench outside for the use of the warders. Despite the proximity of Tower No. 3, while the trees were in leaf the guard stationed there would only catch occasional glimpses of the prisoner on his walks.

We went back into the prison and up the spiral staircase. Opposite Hess's main cell was a similar double cell with a large television set and an old armchair from which he could watch, changing pro-grammes with a remote control unit. However, Charles explained to me that what the prisoner could watch was controlled by the Censors against his submitted selections from a German weekly tel-evision magazine.

We then saw Hess's changing-room and toilet two cells back on the right, his alternative sleeping-cell on the left for hot summer nights, his library cell full of books on the right, his shaving-room on the left with the bathroom next door, and then on back beyond the partition doors to the Duty Chief Warder's office on the left, the Medical Orderly's room opposite on the right (manned by an eld-erly Dutchman), and last on the right, the cell in which all Hess's old clothing was stored, including his leather flying-helmet, fur-lined leather flying suit, and the Luftwaffe captain's uniform in which he had flown to Scotland in 1941.

From there we went to the Mess, where the others had already gathered in the anteroom. Also there to greet me was the British Chief Warder, who was responsible for the catering and running of the Mess in British month. He was a real London Eastender and had been seconded from Her Majesty's Prison Service when the previous incumbent died, remaining on local contract after attaining normal retirement age. In the international atmosphere of this prison, for which his previous service had provided no experience, the poor chap was somewhat out of his depth. He was unable to express him-self clearly enough in English for foreigners to understand him, and any other language was completely beyond him. Consequently he was often misunderstood by the other nationalities, which resulted in constant conflict behind the scenes in British month, the female Mess staff frequently in tears or in a state of rebellion. I myself misunderstood him at first, but eventually appreciated that he was often nervous to the point of being positively agitated, and really had the best of hearts. I was astonished to find that he was a keen runner, and was even taking part in the marathons and 25-kilometre events held in the city, despite his advanced years. His experience in the Prison Service had produced a punctilious sense of security about keys and such like, which at the time seemed superfluous to his role at Spandau but which may have been more pertinent than one then realised. I was later delighted to have to arrange – in my capacity as Protocol Officer – the ceremony at the Ambassador's residence at which he was presented with the Imperial Service Medal.

The Mess, House No. 21, had originally been the Prison Governor's residence and contained some interesting architectural features. Rather like the Administration Block, it had a wide double door as an entrance with a flight of steps leading up to the ground floor. The building was constructed around a square central light-shaft capped by a skylight in the roof, which fed daylight through a sort of sawn-off pyramid through the attic to a more decorative second skylight covering the stairwell above the first floor. On the ground floor a passageway led round the enclosed staircase. First off on the right was the Governors' toilet, then the anteroom, leading into the dining-room on the north-eastern corner of the building, leading in turn to a central serving room with access to the passageway. The warders' dining-room in the north-western corner was separated from the kitchens by the back staircase. Beyond the kitchens, the passage continued past the staff toilets to complete the circuit at the front door.

Upstairs, a similar passage connected the four flag rooms, each with its miniature framed flag – American, British, French, Soviet – on the door. Here one could keep one's duty-free stocks from one national month to the next, use a telephone, and even sleep if necessary, although the furniture and fittings were clearly long disused. There were other storerooms for food stocks and so on in the extensive cellars, and there was also a drivers' and employees' dining-room, for the system provided that anyone employed in connection with the prison was entitled to eat there. This privilege was in fact left over from the immediate post-war years and the Blockade of 1948–9, when food had been a far more vital factor than pay.

The anteroom itself contained a raised bar with foot-rail, cooling facilities, shelves for glasses on the wall behind, pleasant wallpaper but no pictures. There were some brown corduroy-covered armchairs, a couple of coffee-tables, and adjustable lighting over the bar and for the main room.

After a couple of drinks we moved into the dining-room, which was furnished with British Officers'-Quarters-type furniture, three dining-tables run together end to end, flanked by squeaky, black-bottomed chairs. As Chairman, Charles sat at the head of the table with the Frenchman on his right, the Soviet on his left and the American to the right of the Frenchman, the remainder as protocol dictated.

Two waitresses attended the meal, the Governors being served first in the order French, Soviet, American, Chairman, and then the rest. This was the Spandau tradition, maintained until the end. It was said that at one time these luncheons had been quite wild, extended affairs, with wives and girlfriends attending, until they had achieved such a scandalous reputation that the respective military governments had ordered a clampdown, and now only persons directly connected with the administration of the prison were supposed to be invited. However, invitation to luncheon at Spandau was highly prized among all four nations, and the Americans even maintained a waiting list of applicants for the privilege, attendance at hand-over days on the first of the month being the most prized. There were still some items remaining of the cutlery originally issued to the Allied prison, with the prison initials stamped on them, but most had been taken as souvenirs by guests over the years.

We were served a four-course meal accompanied by white and then red wines, after which we adjourned to the anteroom for coffee, served with liqueurs and brandy, thereby establishing a most convivial atmosphere among the diverse personalities. It did not take me long to realise that the Mess was the key to the success of this international operation. Here we could all associate informally and get to know and understand each other better, and so establish a working confidence with which to conduct our more formal business around the conference table. For this, apart from the Berlin Air Safety Centre, was the only place in the Western Sectors of Berlin where the permanently suspicious Soviet military were allowed to mix relatively freely with their Western counterparts.

II

# Changing the Guard

A few days later I went back again to have a more thorough look over the prison. It had been built between the years 1878 and 1881 as a military gaol in a style similar to the other military buildings of that era still to be found in Berlin, using a specially hard-baked brick, a Prussian specification that saw the additional expense in the construction as a saving on future maintenance costs. It was surprisingly modern in concept, with flushing toilets in all the cells, of which there were 132, as well as five condemned cells and twelve dormitories. It is said that French prisoners from the Franco-Prussian War of 1870–1 had assisted with its construction. When the prison was built, Spandau was not a part of Berlin but a separate garrison town of considerable importance, with its own military hospital and several ordnance factories.

The gaol was used as a military detention prison until 1919, after which it came under civil jurisdiction. Then, in 1939, part of the building was turned over to military prisoners awaiting trial, and the rest to political prisoners awaiting transport to the Brandenburg and Sonnenburg concentration camps. An old warder still employed at the time of the Allied takeover in 1946 reported that some 12,000 political prisoners had been executed by guillotine or hanging in the prison during the course of the Second World War. (It has not been possible to confirm this statement.) In 1945 the prison reverted once more to civilian use under British Sector administration, during which time the death penalty continued to be exacted by guillotine. Paper notices in German and English stating prisoners' rights of appeal against sentence were still to be found stuck to the insides of cell doors at the time of the prison's demolition.

Then, during the Nuremberg Trials in 1946, it was decided to set up a jointly-administered prison in Berlin, the only quadripartitely administered city in Germany, for the accommodation of those prisoners who would receive prison sentences, the number not yet being known. The ultimate choice fell on Spandau. The city authorities were ordered to clear the prison of all trace of its former occupants and to furnish whatever materials would be necessary to prepare it for its new role. These preparations were supervised by a major in the Royal Engineers, Freddie Newton, whom I had the good fortune to meet more than forty years later, and consisted basically of isolating the ground floor of the main cell block from the rest of the building, clearing a field of fire and observation outside the walls, erecting an electrified fence around the exterior, and five watchtowers at suitable points on the walls. The guillotine was removed from the execution room, which was then converted into an emergency operating theatre. Later, when the number of prisoners expected was established as seven, Freddie produced a design for a single-storey prison building within a triangular compound, though this idea was not adopted.

Thus, apart from the Berlin Air Safety Centre, this was the sole quadripartite institution to survive the vicissitudes of the Cold War, the Blockade, the Airlift, the crises in Hungary and Czechoslovakia, the Soviet occupation of Afghanistan, and all the other tensions of the forty-five years following the Second World War. In this extraordinary institution the prison warders of four nations worked closely together twenty-four hours around the clock in eight-hour shifts, the Governors met regularly to deal with the various problems that arose, and the walls were punctiliously guarded by the soldiers of each of the four nations for a month at a time in regular sequence.

As mentioned in the last chapter, the chairmanship of the Board of Governors changed monthly and with it went the nationality of the guard, but only three warders were required at any one time, so the three shifts of the day would be provided by the same three nations, the fourth nation being off duty every fourth day in turn.

Looking over the prison in some detail I found none of the spiritual unease one would expect after all the misery and executions that the place had seen there. It was as if it had been exorcised of all of this. Instead, whatever part of the building one went into one always emerged feeling grubby and the first reaction was to go and wash one's hands.

On this occasion I had arranged for the British Chief Warder to show me round. We first went into the Administration Block, where we turned left. The room on the left, dubbed the Chief Warders' Office, contained a couple of ancient desks and, in one corner, a large metal cabinet with a dial on the front, which had once been the nerve centre of the prison alarm system. There was an old, ornate, green-tiled German stove in the room and a sealed door leading off into what had once been a sickbay.

On the other side of the corridor were two rooms containing a mass of junk – old china and the like – the domain of the prison's two handymen. At the end of the short corridor glass-panelled doors gave access to a wide stone spiral staircase connecting the cellars with the chapel on the second floor. We went up to the first floor, which was divided into what in the old days had been classrooms and the prison library. These rooms were strewn with rubbish of all kinds, including old British battledress dyed grey and with the numbers of the seven prisoners superimposed, broken furniture, beds, mattresses, metal pots, china, all long-neglected relics of the past.

On the next floor above we came to the chapel, which extended the width of the Administration Block and most of its length. Massive wooden benches filled the room on either side of a central aisle, facing a wooden wall before which an altar had once stood. A door in this wall gave access to a staircase and the platform above, from which a lectern or pulpit projected centrally over the altar. There was a small gallery on either side of this focal point, and at the very rear of the chapel, an organ loft. The organ looked intact, but was in fact choked with debris from the many pigeons that had taken the place over and which fled in alarm at our approach.

Above the main staircase another flight of steps led up into the attic over the chapel, from which one could get on to the roof through a trap door and look down on the surrounding area.

From there we went down into the cellars. At the bottom of the stairs we came upon the little kitchen in which Hess's food was prepared by his two personal cooks on a combination of an ancient coal-burning stove and a modern domestic electric one.

Further along we came to a steel bunker-type door behind which I was shown two coffins, one in plain deal and one a standard German-style coffin with a proper padded lining. Nearby were the planks and ropes necessary for conducting a burial in the grounds. By this time the idea of burying the prisoner in the grounds had long since been abandoned, but these gruesome relics were still there, no one having the authority to remove them. Beyond, under the Governors' room, was a chapel of rest, stripped bare, with a door to a ramp leading up into the small triangular walled garden between the Archives and the northern wing. This garden was now completely choked with weed-like saplings.

We turned back under the Cell Block. Here the ceiling was vaulted and the cells repeated the pattern of those above. At the cruciform under the tower the brickwork around some old heating ovens built into the structure had been painted red and picked out neatly in white. To left and right, metal staircases led to the storeys above. The Chief Warder pointed to a small trap door in one corner and explained that it was used for the delivery of coke to the boilers, but that it was also planned in an emergency to bring Hess through there from the garden on the sitting stretcher that I had noticed in the Cell Block on my first visit.

Round the corner, beneath the dormitory wing, I was shown the condemned cells. These were the size of the standard cell, but split down the centre by a dense grille in which a door was set. Condemned prisoners barely had space for a narrow, bricked-in wooden bunk with a wooden pillow, and were under constant observation from a warder seated on the other side of the grille. I was shown some of the graffiti scratched in the plaster of the walls above the bunks, some clearly dating back to the post-war period when all kinds of murderous villains had roamed the shattered city.

Next, we went up to the floor above the Cell Block, from where I could see the layout of the interior of the prison as it had been, with yet another gallery of cells above us, each with its individual flush toilet, folding metal-framed bed clamped to the wall, and a metal hand-signalling device to attract the warder's attention. Off the short length of the central corridor between the cruciform and Administration Block were larger cells for four to six persons each, then the wings either side of the cruciform were split longitudinally into dormitories designed for forty men each. At the end of the wings were communal toilet, washing and bathing facilities.

We went back down to Cell Block level, where the Chief Warder unlocked a steel door into the cruciform area. Next to it was another door leading back to the old operating theatre, but the floor of the corridor leading to it was too rotten for us to dare traverse it.

I went out back thankfully into the open air and contacted the guard commander with a view to doing a tour of the grounds and watchtowers with him. He produced a large key to let us through the gates off the courtyard. Working clockwise, we first passed the bricked-up ruin of the old kitchen block with its tall chimney stack, then visited the first two towers. Each tower was equipped with a small searchlight and a telephone, usually supplemented with radio by the unit on guard. The boredom of the job was evident from the constant damage the towers suffered from vandalism by the guards.

Tower No. 3 in the prisoner's garden also suffered from subsidence problems, and had had to be supported by massive struts. There was a prevalent rumour that this tower was haunted, a story perpetuated in order to scare the 'new boys,' and we were later to experience a case of a British soldier firing in terror at what he thought was a ghost, but was probably his own reflection in the glass window.

We completed the circuit of Towers Nos. 4, 5 and 6, passing the fallen-in remains of the old prison hospital before returning to the courtyard through the other gate. I now felt that I knew a little more about my new domain.

Outside the prison walls, I was shown round the rest of the prison grounds. Of the five buildings along Wilhelmstrasse, No. 21 was the Mess, No. 22 partially occupied by prison staff, No. 24 vacant and Nos. 25 and 25A accommodated a couple of bachelor warders. Opposite 25A, encroaching on Smuts Barracks, was a small barrack block used by the British, American and French troops when guarding the prison, but never by the Soviets, who insisted on confining their troops within the walls.

At noon next day, Thursday, 1 October 1981, in my new capacity as British Governor, I attended my first hand-over parade at the prison. The four Governors assembled at the prison a quarter of an hour beforehand to ensure everything was in order. The British guard was already drawn up in two ranks on the left-hand side of the courtyard, with the invited guests under the trees facing them. Just before the appointed hour, the French guard of Gendarmes marched in through the gateway. The British guard came to 'Attention' and went into the 'Present Arms' once the French guard was drawn up facing them. The French guard then returned this compliment, after which the British guard commander declared: 'In the name of Her

Majesty Queen Elizabeth the Second; I hand over responsibility for the security of Spandau Allied Prison!' In his turn the French guard commander declared: '*Au nom du Président de la République Française, j'accepte la réesponsabilité pour la sécurité de la prison alliée de Spandau!*' A key was then handed over between them.

With these courtesies completed, the French guard sergeant led off the rear file of Gendarmes through the left-hand gate, opened for them by the British guard sergeant, to replace the sentries in the watchtowers. Eventually they emerged through the right-hand gate, this time the French sergeant leading the last Gendarme to replace the British Main Gate sentry in the archway, while the British sergeant led his file of relieved sentries to form the rear rank of the British guard.

Once everyone was in position the two guards saluted each other once more, before the British marched off with an 'Eyes Right'. The Governors and those invited to luncheon in the Mess followed through the gate behind them.

Usually present at the ceremony would be the commanding officer and regimental sergeant-major of the battalion providing the British guard, together with the commander and sergeant-major of the company concerned. The colonel of Gendarmerie and two of his officers would represent the French garrison. As the French used their Berlin garrison mainly as a training establishment, the Gendarmes mounted the ceremonial guards for hand-over parades, but conscripts from the training regiments, or sometimes troops from the French garrison in Western Germany, actually guarded the prison for the rest of the month.

The responsibilities of the guard extended only to the external security of the prison, that is, in essence, the manning of the towers. Admittance to the prison was the responsibility of the Main Gate Warder, who held the only set of keys for the entrance. The guard held the keys to the two side gates off the inner courtyard for access to the towers and the inner circuit of the walls. Whenever a civilian working party was allowed into the grounds against a pass signed by the Governors, such as for delivering coke for the boilers, the guard would have to provide an escort. Any contact with the prisoner was strictly forbidden, but the various military units employed there clearly contrived to get as many of their men as possible to catch a glimpse of him.

The Soviet guard that took over at the end of French month came from the 5th Guards Mechanised Infantry Brigade, which formed the Karlshorst garrison in East Berlin. Always very smart, with their Guards insignia and aiguillettes, and their officers in full dress uniforms, they were a great attraction for the tourists watching from across the road as they formed up on the driveway outside the Main Gate, especially when they broke into their spine-jarring goose step.

Whenever the Soviets were present they were accompanied by their Brigade Commander and several officers of his staff. When I first encountered them I was surprised to see that the Brigade Commander was only a lieutenant-colonel, and yet had full colonels on his staff. This baffling arrangement was later explained to me as resulting from officers assigned to a theatre being at the disposal of the commander to employ as he wished. Thus a bright lieutenant-colonel, such as this Durofeyev, could be given a brigade with officers senior in rank to him working for him as staff officers and regimental commanders. Durofeyev's successors were also all lieutenant-colonels.

Durofeyev made a point of the fact that he was Soviet Commandant of Berlin, the first of whom had been Colonel-General Berzarin of the Fifth Shock Army, who is alleged to have been killed in a driving accident shortly after the war ended. In Durofeyev's estimation this made him at least equivalent to the Western Allied brigade commanders, and he would have liked to have met them on equal terms. In due course I gave him the opportunity to meet them by inviting him to the 1982 Queen's Birthday Parade and reception. I arranged places for him and his wife next to the Governors at the rear of the block used for the Diplomatic Corps, where the elevation gave the best view over the parade, held on the Maifeld with its splendid backdrop of the 1936 Olympic Stadium.

Rather to my annoyance, he failed to appear, but when I mentioned this to one of the Soviet External Relations Branch (SERB) guests I was told that he was in big trouble with their Commander-in-Chief, although my informant would not tell me why. It came to light that there had been an unusual event in East Berlin in the middle of the previous night, with Soviet Army troops and armoured vehicles sealing off part of the Unter den Linden. Durofeyev had apparently been practising a contingency plan for the emergency evacuation of the Soviet Embassy without first clearing it with his superiors, and presumably causing considerable political embarrassment for the Embassy *vis-à-vis* the East Germans! He must have had powerful friends, for he kept his job, and even received the Order of the Red Banner with a certificate personally signed by President Brezhnev shortly afterwards. A SERB officer later commented that he could not think what on earth Durofeyev could have done to deserve such an award. Durofeyev also sported a blue medal ribbon with a tiny FDJ (Free German Youth) badge among his decorations, but spoke no German and, like most of his colleagues, was very anti-German in outlook.

The Soviets were always very sensitive about their security. As previously mentioned, instead of using the comfortably appointed barrack block just outside the walls, they kept all their men locked up within the prison walls for their twenty-four shift of duty, using the cramped gatehouse for their accommodation. Their individual sentries were actually locked in their watchtowers, where they would solemnly circle the platform throughout their 'stag' (shift). Their food, mainly consisting of bread and gruel from what I saw of it, was prepared on a stove in a back room, and often there were problems with telephones, power and sewage during their stay.

Communications with their brigade HQ were mainly by means of
radio as the telephone lines were so unreliable at the eastern end.
However, they believed themselves vulnerable and exposed in the
daily bus ride across the British Sector, and once, when Durofeyev
complained about the lack of an RMP escort on a particular day,
he said: 'I can always bring in tanks if you cannot protect us. We still
have our plans from 1945, you know!' His successor, Lieutenant-
Colonel Vladimir Alexandrevich Romanov, clearly did not enjoy
the same patronage, as I saw when I invited him to the Berlin Tattoo,
a spectacular (magnificently directed by Major Michael Parker) held
in the Deutschlandhalle every second year. Romanov turned up in
his best khaki uniform with jackboots, instead of the full parade
uniform worn by the other Soviet guests on what was the BASC/
BRIXIMIS (British Commanders'-in-Chief Mission to the Soviet
Forces in Germany) night for hosting. He received such a wither-
ing glare from the Chief of SERB that he was unable to tackle his
first course, but sat there smoking nervously and only started eating when we had reached our second course. One of the soldiers
employed as a waiter for the evening commented quietly to me as
we rose to go into the spectators' box: 'Bloody hell! Where did you
find that pig, sir?'

Whereas the Western Governors were responsible to their respective Legal Advisers, the equivalent Soviet line of communication
was far more complicated. Liaison with their Embassy was maintained by the Protocol Officer and his deputy, who would invariably
attend the parades, but took no part in the actual administration of
the prison. These, of course, were the very same people that I was
dealing with on the protocol net and thus a useful additional connection. However, the Soviet Governor and his interpreters were
fielded from Potsdam by SERB, who came under the Group of
Soviet Forces in Germany (GSFG). This disparate military chain of
command was to prove awkward when a quadripartite approach to
a problem at diplomatic level was called for. The Soviet military and

diplomats were clearly in two separate camps, with little intercommunication.

In 1981 the Soviet Protocol Officer was the lugubrious Eugen Bogomolov, an obvious KGB man who, when entering a room full of people, had a habit of standing on one side to sum them up. You could see his forthcoming report being rehearsed in his mind. To watch him attempting to do this at a crowded film premiere was quite something! His deputy, Piotr Vinokurov, was on his last tour prior to retirement and had been a mechanic working on Lend-Lease Aerocobra fighter aircraft during the Second World War. In Bogomolov's presence he had little to say, but he could be quite entertaining on the rare occasions he was allowed out on his own. These two were inevitably dubbed 'Boggers' and 'Vino'.

Bogomolov was eventually replaced by Yuri Prontchev, also a member of the KGB, as it turned out, but a person with a good sense of humour and someone it was more often than not a great pleasure to work with. The one sour note occurred after the shooting by a Soviet sentry in East Germany on 24 March 1985 of Major Nicholson, of the American equivalent of BRIXMIS, when Prontchev reduced my female American protocol counterpart to tears with his brutally phrased response to the official protest she was delivering.

On one occasion, when I was researching the 1945 Battle of Berlin, Prontchev was very useful to me. One Friday I had been to the Soviet Army Museum at Karlshorst, where the German capitulation had been signed, and in the museum office had asked permission of one of the officers' wives working there to take some notes from a couple of their exhibits. One was a map in a display case depicting the role of the First Polish Army, and another a map said to have been taken from Hitler's bunker and preserved in a brass-bound glass frame. I had only just started making notes when a soldier tapped me on the shoulder and sent me back to the office, where I was told I would have to wait until the woman director returned. After about

twenty minutes she appeared and went into conference in the inner
office. Eventually she reappeared with the news that I should apply
again in a week's time. When I got back to my office I telephoned
Prontchev and told him what had happened, asking for his help in
getting me clearance.

The following Monday morning Prontchev telephoned back
and asked me to come the next day and bring my camera. Being
a hopeless photographer, this was hardly what I wanted, but armed
with camera and notebook I took the S-Bahn across and met him
outside the Embassy. He was a terrible driver, but I took advantage
of our drive alone out to Karlshorst to ask him what had happened
to produce such a drastic change of mind. He told me that he had
first telephoned the museum to enquire why my request had been
turned down, and was told that they had consulted a colonel responsible for security at GSFG, who had made the decision. He had then
tried this colonel himself without success, so he had spoken to his
Minister, who had told him to ring the colonel the following morning and that would get a different answer, adding: 'If Tony wants it,
he gets it!' Sure enough, a major and a squad of soldiers armed with
hammers and screwdrivers were waiting for us at the museum when
we arrived. I had great difficulty keeping a straight face as they dis-
mantled the exhibition case, then took apart the map frame and slid
the glass out so that I could take my amateurish snaps.

# III

# The Administration

The quadripartite administration of Spandau Allied Prison was based entirely on consensus. The constitution of the administration contained in the Prison Regulations, and to which the Soviets clearly had strict instructions to adhere, quoted the Allied Control Council as the Supreme Executive Authority, with the Allied Kommandatura Legal Advisers forming the Higher Executive Authority to which the Executive Authority – consisting of the Board of Governors (sometimes referred to as Directors) – could refer when necessary. As previously mentioned, the Allied Control Council had collapsed in 1948 when the Soviets walked out, but the 1971 Quadripartite Agreement (QA) had confirmed the three Western Ambassadors at Bonn and the Soviet Ambassador in East Berlin in their responsibilities towards Berlin.

A problem, one which shows the sensitivity of the Governors' role in administering the prison, arose when a trustingly ambitious American Legal Adviser decided to enforce his rights under the terms of the Prison Regulations to enter the prison and visit the prisoner. As American Deputy Governor he already held a permanent pass, renewed monthly with the current Chairman Governor's signature, but hitherto the Western Legal Advisers had not used this pass except in the absence of their own regular Governor, when they sat in as Acting Governors. The furore that this caused, especially as the British were seeking the acceptance of their new female Legal Adviser as Deputy Governor, with the Soviet Governor now refusing to countersign Legal Advisers' passes except in their capacity as Acting Governors, and the Americans not only holding their ground but also claiming the right to sit in on the Governors' meetings if they so wished, nearly brought the administration to a standstill. Eventually common sense prevailed and the Americans dropped their claim, allowing business to continue as usual. The American Governor had been put in a most embarrassing position by his superiors, but had gained the moral support of his colleagues against this outside interference.

Consensus in the administration was everything. If one of the Governors wanted to change anything, innovate anything, all four had to agree, irrespective of who among them was Chairman that particular month. Unilateral action was totally unacceptable.

Each Governor had his own specific field of responsibility. The American was responsible for the Cell Block and the Portakabin, in other words, for the prisoner's accommodation, clothing and provisions. The Frenchman was responsible for the prison finances and liaison with the Berlin *Senator für Justiz* Department, which provided the funds. The Soviet, appropriately, was responsible for labour problems, and myself for the maintenance of the property and external security. However, the actions of the individual Governors in every case remained subject to the formal approval of their colleagues on the Board, and often their co-operation in practice.

For instance, the Soviet Governor was responsible for hiring and firing the non-Allied staff, or UN staff as we often called them, coming from all over the world as they did. Following the usual recruiting and interview formalities, the Soviet Governor would pass me the questionnaires of likely applicants for vetting with the Berlin Police and the security agencies via our Public Safety Branch, and only once this was completed would the names appear before the Board for approval. The security screening could not be as effective as we would have liked, as applicants from Third World countries, in particular, were untraceable outside the city. As an example, the non-Allied staff in January 1986 consisted of:

Internal

    2 secretaries (Zairean/Dutch)

    1 medical orderly (Tunisian)

    2 cooks (Spanish/Portuguese)

    2 handymen (Polish/Greek)

    2 boilermen (E. Guinean/Yugoslav)

External

    2 cooks (Dutch/German)

    3 kitchen helps (2 German/Yugoslav)

    3 waitresses (Spanish/Polish/German)

    1 cleaner (German)

The Board's financial responsibility was considerable. The accounts for 1986, the last normal year of operation, show an expenditure of DM 907,000 on staff pay and DM 503,000 on material items, a total of DM 1,410,000 to be met by the city's *Senator für Justiz* Department and presumably passed on to the Federal Republic as part of the Occupation Costs budget. (These figures excluded the Four Powers' own costs of fielding Governors, interpreters, warders and guards.) The Board was always conscious of their responsibilities in this respect, but with the gradual deterioration of the premises and the ageing of the prisoner some additional expenditure proved necessary from time to time.

For the Governors, getting to know, understand and trust each other was a lengthy business, but obviously of prime importance for a successful administration. The inbuilt suspicions of the Soviets were a major obstacle to be overcome. As previously mentioned, this was mainly achieved in the atmosphere of the Mess once the formal working sessions were over. Gradually a system evolved whereby the comradeship and mutual understanding among the Governors and their interpreters reached a very high peak in the last two years.

In order to conduct an effective meeting, a lot depended upon the order of precedence for that month and whether the Chairman should lead with his comments on a subject or leave them to the end, particularly when testing uncertain ground with the Soviets. On rare occasions the Western Governors met beforehand to discuss the tactics of presentation of a subject to their Soviet colleague, although these tactical discussions in no way involved ganging up on him, for consensus was still necessary before any item of business could go ahead. Another important point that emerged was to present the matter in such a way that the Soviet Governor could report back to his superiors without causing a blow-back.

We gradually evolved a system whereby unless a Governor had received instructions to make a specific statement, or felt strongly that his remarks should be recorded, he would simply note in the minutes beneath the agenda subheading whether it had been approved, rejected, or deferred. However, a statement to be recorded was passed to the Chairman in writing for incorporation verbatim into the minutes. A veto in the form of dissent to a proposal (not necessarily delivered by the Soviet member) automatically torpedoed further discussion, unless a statement had to be delivered and recorded. Whenever a Chief Warder was standing in as Acting Governor, it was customary to refrain, where possible, from dealing with important matters until the return of the principal. This *modus operandi* did a lot to protect the Governors from unnecessary problems with their respective establishments.

However, the acceptance of a proposal, such as for the speeding up of responsive measures to a medical emergency, often required months of patient effort at the conference table. One had to be constantly on the alert for the merest hint of a reaction from one's Soviet colleague that the time was ripe for the acceptance of a carefully worded proposal; on the other hand a careless remark could easily sabotage weeks of preparatory work. Infinite patience was a basic requirement for success, and after some particularly exasperating sessions my interpreter and I could not get away to the Mess quickly enough to unwind.

The nation of the month provided all the provisions for the Mess. As previously mentioned, all those engaged at the prison were entitled to meals while on duty, even the drivers. Except for the Americans, who brought in a cook sergeant and one or two soldiers for the purpose, the Chief Warder of the nation concerned was responsible for running the Mess, thus bringing about a regular change-over in diet and drinks. French months were always a delight, national honour being at stake to provide a memorable cuisine. The Soviets did their best from the rations available to them, but it always was a tough month on the digestive organs. At first the Soviets were well stocked with a variety of vodkas, wines and cognacs, but these vanished almost overnight when the GSFG were subjected to a severe cut in export 'goodies' from the Soviet Union, not even their own cigarettes being available. Czechoslovakian beer and the odd bottle of vodka became all that were available from the bar, although Georgian wine and Crimean champagne were still served at table. The British and American months were generally good in variety, although the censors sometimes suffered during the latter months when the military staff forgot to allow for them.

The Mess also provided a venue for meeting all kinds of people invited or brought along by the hosts. It is time, therefore, to meet the other Governors.

The American Governor, Darold W. Keane, was in his seventies, a short, trim man, proud of his Irish extraction and a keen golfer. He had attained the rank of commander in the US Navy during the Second World War, serving on Admiral Nimitz's staff in the Pacific, and had then gone on to become an Administrative Officer in the State Department. He eventually retired from the service in Berlin, only to be recalled on a part-time basis as the American Governor following the dismissal of Eugene Bird in mid-1972 for abuse of his position (to which I will come in Chapter 4). This supposedly temporary measure had already lasted for over nine years when I arrived. Despite the occasional conflict, I was extremely fond of him and retained a profound respect for the utter integrity with which he approached his work. The pressures on him were obviously intense at times, sometimes stemming from his encounters in the US Mission, but mainly from the behaviour of the Chief Warder he had when I arrived.

This overweight Southern bully-boy, who affected a palpably insincere cordiality, was apparently deeply upset at not being allowed to act as Deputy Governor as his predecessor had been. He took it out on Darold by being thoroughly unhelpful, if not openly disloyal, deliberately causing many problems for his superior with the other Allies, and in doing so arousing their suspicions as to his honesty. He wore the gold badge of a long-term civil servant, however, and could not be fired. Eventually he found promotion out of the city and we were all relieved to see him go.

The French Governor, Michel Planet, was an *Administrateur* with the French Military Government, doubling as their Secretary at the Allied Kommandatura. A year older than me, he had joined the French Foreign Service rather late in his career after an extended independent stay in the United States. He was of a pleasant if slightly taciturn disposition, and spoke excellent English, thus dispensing with the requirement for a French-speaking interpreter for normal business. We understood each other well and got along together without conflict. He would normally be relieved by his Chief Warder when away on leave. During our time together his services were awarded by his government with membership of *l'Ordre National du Mérite*.

Lieutenant-Colonel Gennady Alexseevich Savin was a round-faced, sturdy man in his thirties, not very tall, who had received his promotion only at the beginning of the year. He stuck firmly to the rule book and would sometimes bang the table in anger in debate *à la* Khrushchev, but he also had a ready grin and a sense of humour. He lived in Potsdam with his wife and two young children, and seemed to spend most of his leisure time fishing. It seemed that his appointment was partly due to having been set aside from active duty as a result of some intestinal complaint. He spoke quite fluent German when away from the official conference table, which gave a useful means of direct personal communication, even though my own German was not so fluent. At the same time he had, and tried to conceal, a certain knowledge of English. He too would be relieved by his Chief Warder when away on his annual leave.

In September 1983 Savin was replaced by Major, later Lieutenant-Colonel, Vladimir Alexandrovich Chernykh, a fighter pilot in the Soviet Air Force who had been grounded with back problems resulting from an emergency ejection from his aircraft. He came from Siberia and his first foreign language was French, although again he had some knowledge of English which he tried to conceal. He was a heavy smoker, somewhat nervous of his circumstances at first, but gradually fitted in well and became a good member of the team as his confidence in the rest of us grew. His advantage over the other three of us, like his predecessor, was that his appointment seemed to be full-time, so he could spend far more time at the prison than we could. However, he suffered from being low on the priority list at his local transport pool, and more than once he was embarrassed by ancient staff cars breaking down on him on the way to and from Potsdam via the Staaken crossing-point.

Lieutenant-Colonel Savin had a friend, a Major Yuri Pliev, who wore Artillery insignia and described himself in fluent English as 'another bloody gunner.' Pliev was with SERB at their Zossen office, a jolly, florid-faced North Caucasian with a dark moustache and receding hairline, and a raconteur of endless anecdotes about Georgians and his countrymen of the Caucasus. He claimed to have done his national service with the Soviet Navy at the time of the Cuban missiles crisis (October 1962), which had involved a compulsory extension of his service to five years at sea. As a linguist, and having an uncle who was a full general, he had then found himself a congenial role in the Soviet Army. His attractive wife, Ludmilla, was with him and taught English in a Soviet school. His declared ambition was to found a language school with his wife back in his home town. He was probably either in the military intelligence service (GRU) or the KGB, for he claimed to write the reports of the other members of SERB and was obviously allowed to circulate fairly freely. He was popular with the BRIXMIS officers and their wives, whom he met at Potsdam, and was always a most welcome visitor in our Mess. He left on posting after a while, and then suddenly reappeared – but now as a lieutenant-colonel – three or four years later, returning to the prison as Chernykh's guest. At that time he expressed some concern at the retirement from the Soviet Army of his uncle-protector, but he went on to become a full colonel, working for the Deputy Chief of Staff at HQ GSFG, where he claimed to be a liaison officer to the other foreign armies. I last saw him at the end of 1990, when he invited me to the close-down party given by SERB for their counterparts in the Allied military missions based at Potsdam.

Every month the prison would be inspected by the Inspecting Officer of the nation on guard. For the Western Allies this would be the Sector Commandant accompanied by either his Minister or Political Adviser, for the Soviets the Chief of SERB, Colonel Rubanov and later Colonel Perevertsev, usually also accompanied by either the Minister or Political Adviser from the Soviet Embassy.

The Chairman Governor would greet the Inspecting Officer at the main gate. Then followed an inspection of the guard drawn up in the courtyard. With the Soviets this seemed to entail a lengthy interrogation of each man in turn as to the state of his political indoctrination. When this was over, the Inspecting Officer entered the Administration Block and met the rest of the Governors, who would then escort him to visit the prisoner and tour whatever facilities he wished to see. Hess would be waiting in his cell, wearing a jacket and an open-necked shirt. He would stand near the foot of his bed, his head thrust forward, his eyes missing nothing from under his bushy eyebrows. The Western Commandants sometimes upset the Soviet Governor by addressing the prisoner as 'Herr Hess' or shaking his hand upon leaving, knowing they were breaking the rules and acting rather like naughty schoolboys, thereby provoking a protest to the Chairman Governor at the next opportunity, although never when the culprit Commandant was present.

The inspection provided an excuse for a celebratory luncheon in the Mess, to which a number of guests would be invited. The Chief of SERB always attended at the end of his inspection, but the Western Commandants only rarely.

The monthly Medical Advisers' meeting and examination of the prisoner provided another occasion for a luncheon party. The relationship between the various Governors and their Medical Advisers could be touchy, as the latter resented their medical advice and competence being subjected to the approval of the Board of Governors in matters relating to the prisoner. I had no problems on that score, for I got on well with the various COs of the BMH who filled this role in my time.

A most important element in the administration was the work of the interpreters. The first Soviet interpreter I encountered was Senior Lieutenant Roshkov, a tall young man, fluent in English, German and French. Like the other Soviet interpreters, he appeared to have no proper military training, having been commissioned direct from language school at university. Surprisingly, he claimed to have originally trained for the priesthood, but now had such a profligate reputation for drinking and chasing the female staff around that it was hardy surprising that he and his wife, who was working as a guide at the Cecilienhof in Potsdam, separated at about this time. He was also interested in astrology, and once produced a set of Chinese and Western horoscopes for our entertainment.

The big surprise, however, came when we found Lieutenant Valentina Jakovlova waiting for us in the Mess one day. She was the first female Soviet officer I had seen and was quite attractive, with a trim figure and shoulder-length auburn hair. She had tank insignia on her tunic, which she wore above a knee-length khaki skirt, and her calf-length boots were clearly a recent purchase and non-regulation, for she kept looking down at them and pointing her toes on this first occasion.

Valentina turned out to be the first of a series of females requiring access to the prison proper. She had come with Colonel Rubanov of SERB on his inspection visit. Lieutenant-Colonel Savin, very tongue in cheek, asked us to sign a pass for her, but the Prison Regulations banned females from the Cell Block, so she could not accompany the inspecting officer. Nor was she allowed to accompany the Medical Advisers on their monthly examinations of the prisoner, but otherwise there were no problems about her employment as an interpreter. Savin was very happy to have her on his team, considering her quite an asset, but she fell foul of him when she married an officer at HQ GSFG without first obtaining permission from SERB. Even worse, she failed to invite any of the SERB team to the wedding. Not long afterwards her husband was posted back to the Soviet Union and she went with him.

The Soviet interpreter I was to have most dealings with was Senior Lieutenant (later Captain) Dmitri Naumenko, a very pleasant young officer who was to see us through to the end of the administration as an important member of the team, and whom I met several times later with his wife at either BRIXMIS events or our own events – like the Queen's Birthday Parade or the British Berlin Tattoo – to which SERB were invited.

Our own interpreter had been employed by BMG for decades and was well beyond normal retirement age. His normal role was running the British section of the Allied Travel Office at the Allied Kommandatura, dealing with accreditation of those members of the Eastern Bloc establishments in the city who did not have full diplomatic status. He had a wealth of experience in dealing with the Soviets ever since the Allied Control Council days and was highly respected by them. At the prison he interpreted for all three Western nations, so when he came to retire in the spring of 1982, his departure created quite a problem, particularly as BMG did not wish to finance a replacement.

The Americans decided to provide an interpreter of their own and introduced 'Katya', a delightful and attractive lady who specialised in running tours for Americans in Western Europe and the Soviet Union. Katya had excellent Russian and soon proved a most useful asset to the team, although, again, the Prison Regulations prevented her operating within the Cell Block.

This aspect of the Prison Regulations was put to the test one day when the new Deputy Political Adviser accompanying the French Commandant on his inspection turned out to be a woman. When presented with the pass for signature, none of the Western Governors had commented, although I do not recall having been warned or consulted beforehand, and obviously our Soviet colleague had not noticed, for he expressed his embarrassment at what he considered as a breach of the Regulations when we held our next meeting. Both Darold Keane and I reminded him that this was a changing world, with an increasing number of women in senior diplomatic appointments. We were also able to add that one of Valentina's colleagues, another female interpreter from SERB, had penetrated the Cell Block on one occasion and had got as far as the Duty Chief Warder's Office before being intercepted. Chernykh accepted our argument gracefully and, as mentioned earlier in this chapter, when my next Legal Adviser and Deputy Governor turned out to be a lady, and a very attractive one at that, the only difficulties that arose about accrediting her were not due to her sex.

However, neither I nor BMG were satisfied that we, the British, were properly equipped for the forthcoming rounds of negotiations for the establishment of agreements on procedures for the eventual disbandment of the prison administration. But then an excellent agreement was reached with BRIXMIS for the loan of an interpreter for prison business. At first it seemed that every interpreter on the BRIXMIS strength was taking it in turns to have a go, arousing some caustic comments from the Soviet side, but this soon settled down to a team consisting of a captain and a senior NCO, who between them ensured regular coverage. This was all to the advantage of BRIXMIS as, apart from providing practical experience for their interpreters, it also helped broaden their overall contacts with SERB.

I found the BRIXMIS interpreters extremely useful in developing a better rapport with the Soviets, in spotting important nuances and achieving a clearer understanding of how to negotiate with them. In this, the similarity of the Soviet and British senses of humour proved to be a big advantage. My interpreters were tremendous in their support and we shared a lot in common, including some lasting friendships.

# IV

# Allied Prisoner No. 7

Rudolf Walther Richard Hess was born on 26 April 1894 in Alexandria, Egypt, into a merchant family that stemmed from Wunsiedel in the Fichtelgebirge. His father maintained a strict patriarchal discipline over the household and wielded a strong nationalistic influence. After six years at the local German school, his father withdrew Hess and his younger brother and had them educated at home until 1908, when Rudolf was sent off to school at Bad Godesberg-am-Rhein, near Bonn in Germany. His father's incontestable wish was for him to train for the family business, so he next studied French at the *École Supérieure de Commerce* at Neuchâtel in Switzerland, and then did a business apprenticeship in Hamburg. However, his heart was not in it, and as soon as war broke out in 1914 he escaped his father's domination by volunteering for the Army.

He enlisted at Munich in the 7th Bavarian Field Artillery Regiment, but a few weeks later was transferred to the 1st Company of the 1st Bavarian Infantry Regiment, the so-called List Regiment, which was first engaged at Ypres and then involved in the lengthy battles on the Somme, where it suffered extremely heavy casualties. In April 1915 Hess was promoted to lance-corporal (*Gefreiter*), was awarded the Iron Cross Second Class, and then promoted again to corporal (*Unteroffizier*), all within a month, followed by a further promotion to lance-sergeant (*Vizefeidwebel*) in the October. (Under the German system, the first award for bravery, however outstanding, was the Iron Cross Second Class, the second award the Iron Cross First Class, and so on up the ladder.) During the winter of 1915–16 the regiment was engaged in the fighting in Artois, moving on to the Verdun battlefield in June 1916, where Hess was severely wounded by shrapnel in his left hand and upper arm.

Recovered from this wound, he was posted as a platoon leader in the 10th Company of the 18th Bavarian Reserve Infantry Regiment and sent off to Romania. Once more he was wounded by shrapnel, this time only lightly in his upper left arm, but then, in August 1917, he was more seriously wounded by a bullet that penetrated his chest and left lung before exiting through his back. During convalescence he was promoted lieutenant and decided to try his hand at flying. He attended flying school throughout the spring and summer of 1918, qualifying just in time to take part in the final air battles of the war over Valençiennes in November of that year.

Hess emerged from the First World War an angry young man, brooding over the downfall of his country. He joined the nationalistic, anti-Semitic *Thulegesellshaft* and the *Freikorps Epp*, taking part in the fight against the left-wing Bavarian government, and narrowly escaping being shot as a hostage. In 1920 he enrolled at Munich University to study economics, and attended lectures given by Karl Haushofer, a former major-general turned professor of what he called 'Geopolitics'. Possibly in search of a substitute father figure, Hess struck up a close relationship with this Haushofer. He also spent much of his time in political activities, including the distribution of anti-Semitic pamphlets, and won a prize with an essay on the theme 'How must the man be constituted who will lead Germany back to her old heights?' Then, also in 1920, he first heard Hitler speak, the man who could fulfil his dreams, and hastened to join the Nazi Party.

In 1921 Hess became an active member of the *Sturmabteilung* (SA) and organised a special group of students within the organisation that later came to be known as the *NS-Studentenbataillon* (Nazi Students' Battalion). He then played an important part in the Munich Beer Hall Putsch of 8–9 November 1923, Hitler's abortive attempt to take over the Bavarian government as a prelude to a march on Berlin. When Hermann Göring's armed stormtroopers broke into the nationalist leaders' meeting at the beer hall, Hess's role was to seize the Bavarian government ministers present and detain them at the home of a sympathetic publisher outside the city overnight. He thus missed the march to the Feldherrnhalle and Hitler's precipitate flight. When the news of the failure of the *putsch* reached them, Hess decided to take two of his captives as hostages to a ski hut in the mountains, but lost them on the way when his SA escort drove off without him while he was trying to negotiate overnight accommodation for them. He then made his way back to Haushofer's home, where he was given shelter for several weeks and then assisted to escape to Austria.

In February 1924 Hitler was sentenced to five years' imprisonment in Landsberg Prison, but served only nine months before being released. Meanwhile Hess returned to Munich and was given a light sentence that also sent him to Landsberg. There he took over the role of private secretary to Hitler, recording and participating in the production of the two volumes of rambling monologues that were to form Hitler's *Mein Kampf*. Consequently, when they were released, Hess was appointed Hitler's private secretary and adjutant, thereby wielding considerable influence in the early days of the Party. His full attention was now focused on Hitler, on whom he was in daily attendance. In his fanatical discipleship, he founded the Führer cult and the 'Heil Hitler' greeting that went with it.

In the late 1920s and early 1930s Hess specialised in collecting funds for the Party, including managing the Adolf Hitler Industrial Fund, where he was effective in obtaining considerable donations

from leading industrialists. Based on the Party headquarters at the
Brown House in Munich, his work took him all over Germany, so
he was able to incorporate his love of flying into the business, and
also encouraged Hitler to use this then novel means of transport to
get around the country on his vote-raising campaigns.

Hess's association with Professor Haushofer continued, especially
in connection with the latter's work organising German commu-
nities outside the country, and Haushofer's son, Albrecht, became
Hess's adviser on foreign affairs.

In late 1932 Hess's loyalty to Hitler was rewarded when he was
given charge of a Central Party Commission, which carried considerable powers within the organisation at a time of crisis, the
Nazis having just lost an election. With the Nazi seizure of power
in February 1933, however, Hess's career took another big leap
forward. He became a member of the Reichstag and an honorary
*Obergruppenführer* (general) in the *Schutzstaffel* (SS), whose black uniform with the death's head insignia he wore proudly on all public
occasions, and in April 1933 Hitler went on to appoint him Deputy
Führer of the Nazi Party, 'with the power to take decisions in my
name in all questions relating to the conduct of the Party.' This gave
him a special staff of his own to help supervise all Party offices,
formations and affiliated organisations, with authority to reorganise them and issue rules and regulations as to membership, funds,
activities, and so on. Gradually he brought all associations, clubs and
professional organisations within the country under the Nazi Party's
umbrella and control, banning all independent alternatives. Included
in his achievements at this stage was the creation of the German
Labour Front under Robert Ley, an amalgamation and replacement
of all the trade unions. Hess remained Hitler's intimate, but Martin
Bormann, as Hess's Chief-of-Staff, was gradually able to usurp him
in the increasingly influential and powerful secretarial role.

On 1 December 1933 Hess was appointed Reichsminister without Portfolio, an appointment which was gradually developed to

enable him to participate in the formation of legislation by all departments of the Reich and Länder (county) governments, as well as Hitler's own decrees. Thus Hess was directly involved in a series of laws aimed at opponents of the Nazi regime and at the Jews, including the infamous anti-Jewish Nuremberg Laws of 1935, which led to '*Kristallnacht*' on the night of the 9/10 November 1938, and to increasingly repressive measures being taken against the Jewish population. In the same year his authority was extended down to local council level, with his nominated liaison officers checking on every level of civil administration. By 1937 no government official or Labour Service (*Arbeitsdienst*) officer could be appointed without the consent of Hess or his authorised representative.

During this period of growing power he took a prominent part in the 'Night of the Long Knives' on 29/30 June 1934, when Ernst Röhm, head of the SA, and many of its other leaders were murdered by the SS. Hess had been urging Hitler to take action against Röhm, producing evidence of the insurrection the latter was planning, then acted as a last minute negotiator between them. On the night in question he gave out a list of the names of nineteen persons who were to be summarily executed, and then went on to make a public broadcast justifying the action taken against the leadership of the SA. At the same time, other rivals within the Nazi Party were shot, as also were a number of prominent non-Nazis. One source reports that Hess and Göring were among the main executioners of Röhm's group. Subsequently Hess went on to reorganise the SA with SA Chief-of-Staff Viktor Lutze.

However, 1934 also saw the nomination of Göring as Hitler's successor, while Hess remained Hitler's personal Deputy, a clear indication of how the leader's favours were turning.

In 1938 Hess was appointed a member of the Secret Advisory Council, which had been set up to advise Hitler on matters of foreign policy. In this capacity Hess devised a scheme for the assassination of the German Ambassador to Austria, Franz von Papen, by

German agents posing as Austrian patriots, thus giving the necessary pretext for Nazi interference. However, the Austrian police found a copy of the plan (the so-called 'RH document') in a raid on an illegal Nazi base in Vienna and tipped off von Papen.

Then, on 30 August 1939, just two days before the invasion of Poland, Hess was appointed one of the six members of the newly-constituted Ministerial Council for the Defence of the Reich, which was equipped with supreme legislative and executive powers for the unified direction of the government and economy in the defence of the Fatherland. The power of the council extended down to the regional administrative level, where the local *Gauleiter* was usually appointed Reich Defence Commissioner with authority to co-ordinate all defence activities.

After the conquest and division of Poland (under the secret Nazi-Soviet Pact of August 1939, eastern Poland went to Russia) in the first half of September, Hess became involved in the administration of the occupied territories and the formulation of penal laws against their inhabitants, based on the premise that the Pole, being a Slav and therefore in Nazi eyes an *Untermensch* (sub-human), was less susceptible to the infliction of ordinary punishment than other human beings. He also assisted Himmler in recruitment for the SS, which was now fielding the infamous extermination squads, and in the expansion of the Waffen-SS as an élite fighting force created to mirror the Nazi image of a German superman.

The foregoing shows the power that Hess had accumulated in the period leading up to the outbreak of war, and the highly important role he had played in preparing the German people for what Hitler wanted of them. This in itself was a considerable achievement, effectively unifying the whole life of the country behind Hitler. Photographs taken during this period of the government front bench in the Reichstag, then sitting in the Kroll Opera House, show Hess gradually moving up to the seat next to Hitler. Under Hess's personal direction the doubters, the innocent, and the silent opponents of

Hitler had all been enmeshed in the sinews of the Nazi state. Outright protesters and potential opponents had been, and were being, dealt with by the SA, SS, the Gestapo and other police forces, and the concentration camps. Then the lightning German victories of 1939 and 1940 put an end to any remaining indifference among the mass of the population with a surge of national pride. The way was now clear for all the evil that was to follow under the Nazi banners.

In short, Hess had shown himself to be, as Bernard Levin later put it, 'a profoundly evil man, justly convicted and condemned ... at Nuremberg.'

1941 saw the peak of arrogance among the Nazi leadership. Anything was possible, nothing was beyond their grasp. The planning for the invasion of the Soviet Union was well under way, and the Wannsee Conference of January 1942 introducing the 'Final Solution' for the elimination of the Jewish population of Europe was just round the corner.

If we look at the Nazi élite gathered around Hitler at this time, we see that the principal figures had each established their own individual empires: Göring with his Luftwaffe and the enormous industrial influence and wealth gained under the Four-Year Plan; Himmler with his SS and police; Goebbels with the media and film industry. Despite his achievements, however, Hess, the Deputy Party Führer, was now the odd man out and, as Hitler became more and more preoccupied with the conduct of the war and the expansion of his empire eastwards, Hess's influence with him began to wane. What could he do to regain his beloved leader's favour?

On 19 July 1940 Hitler had made a speech in the Reichstag offering peace to the British Empire, saying that only a small clique of British warmongers were keeping the war alive, while all that the British people wanted was peace.

Hess later admitted to Lord Simon, the Lord Chancellor in Churchill's government, that his idea for his flight to Britain originated at about this time.

Felix Kersten, Himmler's doctor and confidant, also treated Hess, and was interrogated by Reinhard Heydrich after Hess's flight, as were all those others who had had connections with him. Kersten later wrote: 'He was firmly resolved to stake his life on a great deed in the service of Germany.' He also wrote:

> The world must come to see that Germany is unconquerable. And he, Hess, had to stretch out his hand, to bring about a reconcilia-tion between Germany and the other nations. Another time he told me that he had to concentrate all his powers and harden himself – he needed all his strength for the deed which would secure the salvation of Germany. When I asked him what he meant by this 'sal-vation,' Hess replied that he could not tell me, but he was preparing for an act of historic importance.

Hess certainly knew of Hitler's plan to invade the Soviet Union, being regularly briefed, in his capacity as Deputy Führer and member of the Council of Ministers for the Defence of the Reich, by General Walter Warlimont of the Operations Staff of the *Oberkommando der Wehrmacht* (HQ Armed Forces).

Hess's own secret plan was to secure the way for Germany's expansion to the east by neutralising the British opposition with a peace treaty. Such a coup would surely prove his worth to his Führer and recover his position at Hitler's side.

Hess had continued to keep up his flying. In 1934, inspired by Charles Lindbergh's famous solo flight across the Atlantic in May 1927, he had even won the annual air-race around the Zugspitze, Germany's highest mountain. Then at the beginning of the war he had wanted to fly with the Luftwaffe at the Front, but Hitler for-bade this, wanting him to give up flying for good. Eventually Hess promised not to fly for a year, but when the year was up he secretly resumed flying with the aid of contacts in the air industry. So it was that he was able to have a Messerschmitt 110 (a twin-engined fighter-bomber) fitted out with special long-range tanks and placed at his disposal at Augsburg for training flights, until, on 10 May 1941, circumstances were sufficiently favourable to attempt his flight to Scotland, a flight that stretched both the aircraft and the pilot to the full extent of their capabilities.

This 900-mile flight took him north-west out of Augsburg and along the Rhine as far as Holland, where he turned 90 degrees east as far as the mouth of the River Ems before resuming a north-westerly course that brought him to within 125 miles of the Scottish coast. His plan was to land at last light on the landing strip at Dungavel House in Lanarkshire, the home of the Duke of Hamilton, but he had miscalculated the length of daylight at that latitude and so circled around a while before heading for the coast at Bamburgh and then crossing over to the west coast. He had memorised the route and found the bearings he was looking for, but not the landing strip. Consequently he had to resort to his parachute, injuring an ankle in the process.

Meanwhile, Hess's adjutant, Karl-Heinz Pintsch, had been tasked with delivering his long letter of explanation to Hitler at the Berghof, near Berchtesgaden. The question of whether Hitler knew or did not know of Hess's flight has been a subject of debate ever since, but recently an interesting link in the chain of pertinent evidence came to light in my presence. After a press conference on 28 August 1992, opening a debate on the future of the drivers' bunker found on the site of the Reichs Chancellery garden, Herr Rochus Misch, a former sergeant in the Waffen-SS '*Leibstandarte Adolf Hitler*' (the Führer's 'bodyguard' division), who was the switchboard operator in the Führerbunker during the siege of Berlin, volunteered the information that he had served on Hitler's personal entourage as bodyguard, courier and servant for several years. He said that one of his roles was to hand Hitler important dispatches, which the latter would read in his presence and, if he wanted them destroyed, would then tear in half before returning them to Misch for shredding. He distinctly recalled the arrival of Hess's letter to Hitler, delivered after the Deputy Führer had taken off for England. Hitler read the letter without comment, exclamation or change of expression, tore the letter in half and silently handed it back for destruction.

Although this might give the impression that Hitler knew about the plan all along, it seems more likely that the intentions expressed in Hess's letter were in fact fully in keeping with his own line of thought. He had been reluctant to engage Great Britain all along, for his ambitions lay essentially within the European landmass. The dissipation of his forces to the Mediterranean area in support of his floundering Italian ally's campaign against the British, when he really needed them for the conquest of the Soviet Union, could not have been all that welcome. However, Hess's effort was a gamble, and when it failed to evoke a favourable response from the British government Hitler had no option but to disclaim the attempt. His Deputy, he said, must have been temporarily insane to have attempted such a flight.

Of course, what this arrogant Nazi leadership failed to realise, cosseted by the adulation that surrounded them, was how the rest of the world regarded them. Certainly in Britain they were seen as a gang of highly dangerous and unscrupulous criminals, whose uniforms and posturings added a touch of the ludicrous, as was so beautifully caricatured in Charlie Chaplin's film *The Great Dictator.* Consequently Hess's arrival in the United Kingdom was treated at first with incredulity, and when he tried to put forward his case he was simply 'laughed out of court.' Churchill ordered him to be 'put on ice,' in fact treated as he would have been as a senior prisoner of war but in isolation from others, until such time as he could be brought to trial as the criminal he was. Meanwhile Nazi Germany had to be defeated.

So Hess had to sit out the rest of the Second World War at various locations in the United Kingdom, the news of his arrival no more than a 'seven-day wonder.' The various interrogations he was

**1. & 2. Soviet Guard Preparing to take over.**
Top picture shows barrack block used by Allied guards during their duty months. The bottom picture shows the Main Gate used by the Soviet guards for their accommodation.

3. Aerial view of Prison taken shortly after Hess's death, with the new perimeter fence and gate installed.

The ruins of the old prison laundry with its chimney can be seen on the left with the disused workshops behind. Hess's lift is hidden by the trees left of the main cell block. The ruins of the prison hospital can be seen bottom right and part of Brooke Barracks top right.

**4. & 5. Watching a parade**

**Above**: Lt Col Savin, Tony Le Tissier, the Adjutant of the 2nd Bn The Royal Irish Rangers, Lt Col Durofeyev, Michel Planet and Darold Keane on 1 July, 1984.

**Below**: Michel Planet, Gendarmerie Lt Col, Captain Francis Hobbs (ADC to GOC), Tony Le Tissier, Lt Col Chernykh, Lt Col Rory Forsyth and some officers of the 1st Bn The Prince of Wales's Own Regiment of Yorkshire on 1 February, 1983.

**6. & 7. East–West relations**
Tony Le Tissier sharing a joke with Yuri Prontchev and a colleague from the Soviet Embassy.

8. Adjourning to the Mess after a Parade.

9. The Main Building seen from the top of the Mess, the administration Block with the chapel above, the Tower over the cruciform centre of the Cell Block and a dormitory wing. Tower No. 6 and the ruins of the prison hospital are in front.

10. The Governors' Mess, No. 21 Wilhelmstrasse.

11. Hess in the second position on the cabinet bench at a session of the Reichstag held in the Kroll Opera, enraptured by his Führer.

**In the Mess**
12. **Above**: Lt Col Savin with Valentina.

13. **Below**: Majaor Yuri Plaiv, Tony Le Tissier and Lt Col Gennady Savin.

subjected to yielded little of value, and his subsequent behaviour in captivity was to attract the attention of a succession of psychologists. (This curious behaviour, however, had ceased long before I came into the picture.)

The Nuremberg Trials of 1945–7 have come in for criticism as 'victors' trials,' but it is clear that every attempt was made to bring about a fair judgement in what proved to be a unique situation. How else should such people have been treated? Under the rules of the game then established, Hess was only awarded a life sentence by the American, British and French judges, whereas the Soviet judge demanded the death penalty, the three-to-one majority ensuring from the Soviet side that there would be no reprieve, no remission of sentence in the years to come.

Significantly, Hess said in his final statement to the Nuremberg court: 'I am happy to say that I have done my duty towards my people, my duty as a German, as a National Socialist, as a loyal follower of the Führer. I regret nothing.'

When the batch of seven prisoners eventually arrived at Spandau Allied Prison, a deliberate point was made of humiliating Hess by treating him last and giving him the lowest number, Allied Prisoner No. 7. That he remained an arrogant, awkward and troublesome inmate is testified to by Albert Speer in his book *Spandau: The Secret Diaries* and by all the other prisoners whose complaints against him were recorded in the prison records.

The other six prisoners were No. 1, Baldur von Schirach, head of the Hitler Youth, who was to serve a 20-year sentence; No. 2, Grand Admiral Karl Dönitz, head of the German Navy from 1943 and Hitler's successor as head of state, who was to serve a 10-year sentence; No. 3, Baron Constantin von Neurath, who had been Foreign Minister from 1932–8, then Governor of Bohemia and Moravia, and had a 15-year sentence but was released on grounds of ill health in 1954 and died in 1956; No. 4, Grand Admiral Erich Raeder, head of the German Navy until 1943, who had a life sentence, but was released on grounds of ill health in 1955 and died in 1960; No. 5, Albert Speer, Minister of Armaments and Munitions, who was to serve a full 20 years; No. 6, Walther Funk, Minister of Economics, also with a life sentence but who was released on grounds of ill health in 1957 and died in 1960. This then was my charge on behalf of the British government when I took over my appointment on 1 October 1981. I received no specific briefing about Hess, only what little Charles had to say. It was presumed that I knew what to do, and I presumed that I knew what to do. The question of the Prison Regulations by which we were supposed to operate did not arise until much later, when the Soviet Governor referred to them as his guidelines in some matter we were contesting. As far as I was concerned, Hess simply had to be looked after as humanely as possible within the circumstances of his imprisonment. Clearly any improvements would be a bonus, and equally clearly there was room for some. So I had a job to do.

My contacts with the old man I kept fairly brief and businesslike. Basically this was an evil man, whose crimes against humanity fully justified the punishment he had been awarded, yet I could readily sympathise with his problems of contending with old age and his continued isolation from persons with whom he could communicate freely. At the same time I could see that he was probably receiving far more care and attention than the majority of people of his own age, and that he was still able to maintain his personal dignity. Nor did he suffer from any of the anxieties and stresses imposed by modern life that I have witnessed among elderly people. My distinct impression was that he had become conditioned to his circumstances and was relatively content.

More often than not he would be eating his extended lunch when I visited him, as that would be the time at which I would have to be at the prison anyway. I would always knock on his cell door before going in. He would be sitting up in his hospital bed with a napkin round his neck, working his way through a series of covered dishes kept warm on a hot-plate. Normally he would react as if he was quite glad to see me. I would ask him how he was that day and whether he had any particular wishes, which usually turned out to be something in connection with his correspondence, letters that had not arrived or which he wished to refer to. Sometimes it was a complaint or a bizarre request of some sort, such as for a new alarm clock, a new medicine, or even a pacemaker, as happened on one occasion. He quite liked discussing the soccer and tennis he had seen on television, but these were subjects that have always failed to interest me, so I was not much use as a collocutor there. He was not above trying harmless games with us, playing one Governor off against another, but his sense of humour was more pedantic than ready to hand, and in his letters he would insert '*Lachen*' to indicate a humorous bit. I never posed him any questions about his past, nor do I think he would he have replied if I had done so.

This had happened, however, on a wide scale in the time of a previous American Governor, Eugene K. Bird. He had apparently taken advantage of his office in order to interrogate Hess privately with a view to producing his book, *The Loneliest Man in the World*, and to becoming the media consultant on the whole subject of Hess and the prison. Bird had, apparently, even obtained Hess's co-operation in his project on the understanding that the prisoner would be able to edit the result. This Hess had done but, as I understand it, that edited version was not the one that was eventually published. It was not my intention to emulate this 'Born-Again Christian', who had been rightly dismissed from his post for these unauthorised and highly irregular activities.

Easily the most bizarre allegation made about Hess was Dr Hugh Thomas's contention that Allied Prisoner No. 7 was not the true Rudolf Hess but a substitute; 'my uncle Itzik,' as Bernard Levin put it. Dr Thomas had published his book *The Murder of Rudolf Hess* well before I became the British Governor, calling upon all sorts of prominent people to support his ridiculous theory and generally creating quite a lot of mischief that was to continue over the years.

In reality, contrary to what he implied in his book, Dr Thomas had never had direct access as a doctor to Hess during his time at the BMH. His two brief encounters had both been in the dimly lit Radiological Department as an unauthorised bystander while Hess was being X-rayed. His learned medical observations from that point on appear to have been based on what he saw in the dim light of that room and on a purloined X-ray, for he would certainly not have had any legal right to examine that X-ray or have it in his possession.

In 1983 a letter was received from the *Institut für Zeitgeschichte* (Contemporary History) in Munich, an eminently respectable establishment, saying that they had been sent anonymously an X-ray photograph that had 'No. 7, BMH Berlin' and the date '25 Nov 69' printed on the bottom strip. Commenting on this X-ray after its return to its rightful owners, the then Commanding Officer of the British Military Hospital said that it had been folded, apparently as a means of smuggling it out of the hospital.

That same CO was tasked with checking out Dr Thomas's allegations both for the record and to meet the inevitable questions raised in the House of Commons. Dr Thomas had apparently researched Hess's medical history from his First World War military records. Although there was no trace of a wound on any of the chest X-rays taken between 1965 and 1979, this was explained by the wound path being so close to the mid-line that any fibrosis present would have been obscured by the heart shadow.

Following a full examination of Hess made at the BMH on 16 May 1979, the CO reported that all the entry and exit scars that Dr Thomas denied existed were there, just as expected. He then went on to criticise the inaccuracy of some of Dr Thomas's arguments, which clearly showed the latter's lack of knowledge of First World War casualty conditions, including problems being 'caused by the lack of antibiotics' that had yet to be discovered!

Among the correspondence that came my way were two letters from a Dublin journalist, asking for certain information from me as British Governor for an article he was writing. They were the most badly typed and presented letters I have ever seen, and must have been bashed out on a really ancient machine. It was set policy to ignore all such requests and they usually went straight into the shredder, but I could not resist withholding the photocopy of one letter he had attached. This priceless gem read as follows:

Albert Speer

Heidelberg 11.2.1980

Dear Mr Anally,
I became familiar with a British Army expression while I was in Spandau: B.B.B. (Bullshit Baffles Brains) and this is my answer to Dr Thomas' claims.
Yours sincerely,

ALBERT SPEER
6900 Heidelberg 1
Schloß-Wolfsbrunnenweg 50
Tel.26501

# V

# Conditions

What was it like for Hess, the solitary prisoner in Spandau Allied Prison? When he first arrived with the other six major war criminals convicted at the Nuremberg Trials the regime was indeed very rigorous for all of them. Life in the prison at that time was perhaps best described by Albert Speer in his *Spandau: The Secret Diaries*. However, following the release of Speer and Baldur von Schirach on 30 September 1967, the plight of the then seventy-two-year-old Hess, the sole remaining prisoner, attracted worldwide sympathy, and brought pressure on the Western Governors to ameliorate his living conditions.

Until this time, throughout twenty-eight years of captivity, he had steadfastly refused to accept any visitors. Then, in November 1969, he suddenly stopped eating and suffered a serious loss of weight. Despite his extreme reluctance he was taken for examination to the nearby British Military Hospital, where evidence of a healing perforated ulcer was found. His wife and son were informed of the matter and promptly requested permission to visit him, but again Hess bluntly refused their request. However, he must have been giving the matter some thought, for not long afterwards he surprised everyone by writing a request to the Governors asking them to allow his wife and son to visit him so that they could eat a Christmas dinner together. The latter part of the request could not be met, but the first visit of half an hour took place on 29 December 1969, and was to set a new pattern for the future.

The first major ameliorations in conditions followed Hess's suicide attempt in February 1977. These were summarised in a paper written by the then British Governor, George Marshall, in December 1978, which gave a fairly accurate picture of the situation that existed when I arrived on the scene three years later. The changes in respect of the 1947 Prison Regulations, which had been amended in 1954 for the only time, reflected a considerable achievement during the course of the previous two years of George's office, as some senior British official had commented: 'Given the French disinterest in Hess, and the complete lack of effectiveness on the American side, these achievements are all to the credit of George's initiative and skill in handling the Russians.'

George himself commented that to get improvements in Hess's conditions it was necessary to take things along bit by bit, and whenever possible informally. Once something was recorded in the minutes of the Governors' meetings, it was out of the Soviet Governor's hands, as we were well aware. However, the French and American Governors could also prove difficult at times, with remarks to the effect that we were running a prison and not an old people's home.

In describing the conditions in which Rudolf Hess lived during my time as the British Governor, the first thing is to eradicate the impression of 'solitary confinement,' the expression so often used in the media and elsewhere, and which could not have been further from the truth. Within the Cell Block in which he lived, he could and did move about freely between the cells allocated to him for various purposes and could communicate equally freely with the warders on duty and the medical orderly. With the exception of the library, clothing store and dispensary, none of these cells were locked.

The heating of this area was adjusted to whatever temperature he requested, and he set his own routine, usually rising early to bath and shave, and sleeping often during the day. As already related, he prepared his own menus for implementation by the two cooks especially employed for him, and he consumed an extraordinary amount of food for a person of his age.

Whenever he wished to go into the garden, which was generally twice a day, for it was his favourite place, for obvious reasons, he would inform the escorting warder in advance and then take a considerable time preparing himself, always wrapping himself up well, even in warm weather. Hess, prepared for the garden in winter, with several layers of clothing under his coat, balaclava, scarf, hat, gloves and moonboots, was truly an extraordinary sight.

The improvements in his living conditions that occurred in my time, as in George Marshall's, I can claim were again all due to British initiatives. Shortly after my arrival, the Medical Orderly, an elderly Dutchman who had been there since the beginning and was well past retirement age, was replaced by a Tunisian, Abdallah Melaouhi, a tall male nurse trained in German hospitals and married to a German, and who himself spoke both French and German. Hess took exception to his colour at first, but soon gained confidence in his gentle skills. Melaouhi attended him with great conscientiousness, carefully supervising every move, his early-morning baths, his exertions on an exercise bicycle in the dispensary, and massaging him, assisting him to dress and giving him every possible personal attention. Melaouhi was given an apartment in House No. 22, just outside the Main Gate, and so was always readily available in an emergency, and whenever he was away on leave arrangements were made with the BMH to provide male military nurses to replace him.

George Marshall was the first to raise the possibility of installing a lift to provide easier access to the garden than that afforded by the spiral staircase. The original idea was to replace one with the other, but this was eventually dropped because of the fire risks involved in installing such a lift in the spiral staircase's location, the upheaval the installation would cause and the time and trouble it would take, bearing in mind the thickness of the vaulted ceiling to the cellar below.

Nevertheless, the problem remained that one day Hess would no longer be capable of using the spiral staircase, and it would then be necessary to push him out in a wheel-chair from his living accommodation behind thick walls half a floor up from garden level. Eventually I hit on the idea of using the empty cell between his bedroom and toilet as a passageway to a lift that could be built outside in the garden. The Public Services Agency (PSA) produced plans and costed the project at about DM 130,000 (roughly £50,000 at the time).

Michel Planet and I then went round to see the official in the *Senator für Justiz* Department responsible for the prison finances, explained our proposal and the reasons, and, somewhat to our surprise, immediately obtained the additional financing required. The lift, produced in magnificent style, was large enough to contain a stretcher. It was powered by a hydraulic system installed in the cellars, and operated very smoothly. The installation caused very little disturbance, a hole being knocked through the external wall below the window of the empty cell to accommodate a door, and then a steel ramp and handrail were built into this improvised passageway to assist movement to and from the lift. Outside, a little area was fenced off with sheet-metal panels, and concrete pathways were laid leading through a door into the prisoner's garden, with further concrete paths and railings leading to his normal exercise area.

Hess's exercise path, which had deteriorated over the years, I had the Royal Engineers re-lay so that he had a smooth, well drained surface to walk on. Having tried the lift once or twice, he then declared that he preferred to use the spiral staircase for exercise while he could, so the lift became 'Le Tissier's Folly' for a few months until he decided that it was the best route after all.

Another improvement, this time to his diet, arose one day when I looked in to see if he needed anything. As usual, he was working his way through a copious lunch. When he complained about the poor quality of the milk he was getting, I suggested he might try the Danish milk supplied to the NAAFI, which reminded me very much of the Guernsey milk I had been brought up on. He tried some and liked it, so thereafter I arranged for a regular supply to be delivered by the Toc H canteen van as it passed by on its rounds of the various barracks.

Other items included the replacement of his hospital bed with a lower, and thus safer, type, the wall-to-wall carpeting of his bedroom and television cells, the slip-proofing of the steps on the spiral staircase, the modification of his cell doors so that they could be opened from the inside, and the installation of a shower stall and more safety grips in the bathroom.

On another occasion, Hess asked for a replacement for his Loden greatcoat, which was of considerable thickness and weight. The question of clothing was a difficult one, and Darold Keane had been given many a hard time in the past by the prisoner when selecting items for him. Someone came up with the idea of providing a quilted coat, Hess having commented favourably on one worn by a Soviet warder. A chocolate-brown one was obtained on approval and Hess liked the idea of the tremendous saving in weight, but it was too short for him. He wanted something that would cover him down to the ankles, so eventually a tailor was found who would improvise an extended padded skirting to the basic garment, which proved acceptable to our pernickety charge.

In July 1985 I presented a list of proposals on behalf of the three Western Allies for the consideration of the Soviet Governor, with a view to increasing Hess's visiting and correspondence privileges, and even raising the possibility of his being able to speak with his invalid wife by telephone. These proposals had been worked out by the Legal Advisers, that about the use of a telephone coming direct from the American Sector Commandant. In view of the attitude of the Soviets at that time, however, I had little confidence in success. They were reviving memories of their sufferings in the Second World War, commemorating 1985 as the fortieth anniversary of their defeat of Nazism, and we had already been told that we could expect no special concessions for Hess that year.

Inevitably, these proposals were rejected, but the following April I returned to the charge with those concessions with which I thought we had a chance of succeeding, the doubling of Hess's visiting and correspondence allocations. One month later Chernykh made a statement agreeing to these proposals 'as an exception to the existing rules without the introduction of any kind of alteration to the regulations,' and reserving the right, 'in case of emergency, to raise the issue for returning to the rules currently in force and fixed in the regulations of the Prison.' It was agreed that the head of the Hess family, the prisoner's son Wolf-Rüdiger Hess, would be informed by one of the prison secretaries by telephone and that I, as Chairman, would inform the prisoner, but that nothing would be committed in writing to the family.

Andrea Hess, Wolf-Rüdiger's wife, immediately wrote back asking for these changes to be put in writing, and then sent a second letter asking whether they were the prisoner's idea, both these letters being ignored by common consent among the Governors. Hess set out the changes in his next letter to his family, which the Censors then insisted be rewritten omitting the offending passage. However, there had been some misunderstanding in the translations, for it later transpired that the Soviets would only actually allow one adult in with the prisoner at a time, although the timing could be flexible.

In the end these proposals came to nothing, for the family were either unable or unwilling to take them up.

The last physical improvements involved the purchase of an adjustable armchair with a combined footstool to replace the worn-out armchair in the television cell, and a table for eating or writing purposes in Hess's main cell.

Other welfare facilities available to Hess included a film projector for showing home-movies of his grandchildren, and also a record-player used by the chaplains to entertain him with classical music during their weekly visits.

# VI

# The Family

Certainly, providing moral support for the prisoner must have imposed a considerable burden on the family. Apart from the weekly letter to Hess, most commonly provided by either Ilse, his wife, or Andrea, his daughter-in-law, there was the question of the monthly and Christmas visits to be met. None of the family lived in Berlin and therefore, because of the difficulties of traversing the German Democratic Republic to and from West Berlin, they had to fly in for the day from various parts of the Federal Republic, entailing considerable expense in air tickets and taxi or car hire.

The business of censorship of the prisoner's incoming and outgoing mail was delegated to the British and Soviets, most of the work being done by the interpreters. (Both the Soviet Governors in my time took the opportunity of collecting the postage stamps for their children.) Around Christmas and Hess's birthday a vast amount of mail would arrive addressed to him from all over the world, all of it being examined and then shredded, as Hess was only allowed one letter per week from a member of his family, and allowed to despatch only one himself. One item I intercepted was a homemade Christmas card from Colin Jordan, the one-time English fascist. This incorporated photographs of Jordan and his house near Harrogate, and was stamped with an emblem comprising the basic elements of earth, water, air and fire. There was also a constant supply of pseudo-Nazi material from Illinois.

Included in this process was the censorship of television programmes. As soon as the weekly German television magazine was published, Hess would get a copy to study and mark the programmes he would like to see. We would then go through the selection, striking off those about either the Nazi era or himself. The amended copy would then serve as a guide for the supervising warders.

He was not supposed to watch current news programmes, but as he received a variety of newspapers, albeit censored on the same basis, this always seemed a little ridiculous to me, even if it was actually applied in practice. With a modern sophisticated television set covering all the channels available in Berlin from both East and West, there was certainly a variety of programmes – and opportunities for him to defy the censorship – available to him at the touch of a button on his remote-control unit.

The question of the censorship of newspapers was often a vexed one among the Governors. Between us we provided a variety of German newspapers, including *Neues Deutschland* from East Germany, and these were censored daily by the prison secretaries. But the Americans supplied the *Frankfürter Ailgemeine Zeitung*, and insisted that this was to be censored by themselves, which gave rise to some heated debates with the Soviets, often lasting weeks, over instances such as when the copy of the newspaper containing Wolf-Rüdiger's full-page advertisement for the '*Lasst Hess frei*' campaign went into the Cell Block.

When Chernykh took over and first mentioned this problem, I told him that he should first read the minutes on the subject from Savin's time, and then give me ample notice so as to enable me to apply for leave beforehand. He laughed but raised the subject later nonetheless, and we went into yet another protracted series of heated discussions between the two factions.

Hess was allowed a visit of one hour per month throughout the year, with an extra visit of one hour allowed in December. These visits were limited to members of his family, that is his wife Ilse, who continued to suffer from ill health (I only saw her once on the occasion of her last visit on 21 October 1981), his sister, Frau Margarethe Rauch, and his sister-in-law, Frau Inge Pröhl, both game old ladies, neither in the best of health but quick-witted and determined to play their part. His nephew Wieland Hess came once or twice, as did another nephew, Michael Hess, and a niece, Monika Hess, but most visits were either from his son, Wolf-Rüdiger, or his daughter-in-law, Frau Andrea Hess. I think the latter gave him the most pleasure, prattling away about her three children and producing photographs and home-movies of their exploits, for which a projector was available. Wolf-Rüdiger would talk about technological developments and such, subjects that also interested the old man.

The Visiting Room was square, and split in half by a floor-to-ceiling screen with a large opening cut in the centre above narrow tables placed on either side. Once the visitor had arrived the Governors or their representatives would sit round the sides of the room and the prisoner would be brought in by a warder. Greetings would be exchanged, then the warder would help Hess to settle down comfortably in his chair on the far side of the screen, with his feet up on another chair and a blanket over his legs. The visitor would sit opposite. At the end of the hour the warder would call time and the visitor would be escorted back out to the Main Gate. Rather than try to listen in to the conversation, I would usually spend my time catching up on private correspondence.

Requests for visits from the family had to be received about ten days in advance to ensure that the request was approved at a regular Governors' weekly meeting and the reply sent back in time for the visitor to make the necessary travel arrangements. Upon arrival, visitors had to sign a certificate to the effect that they would not divulge anything to the media about the visit. Wolf-Rüdiger con-

sistently broke this rule, however, and consequently had permission
for at least one visit revoked and transferred to another member of
the family.

On 17 March 1984, Wolf-Rüdiger wrote to the Governors
requesting special arrangements for a visit on his father's forthcoming ninetieth birthday. He wanted to bring his wife, eldest daughter
and son and for them to have two hours alone with his father, without supervision, in the Governors' Conference Room rather than in
the normal Visiting Room. Allowance for the visit of a child under
sixteen years of age when accompanied by an adult was found in the
rules, but on 28 March, before the matter could be fully discussed
among the Governors, Andrea Hess came on an authorised visit
during which she mentioned these proposals to her father-in-law.
Darold Keane then passed round a note among the Governors supervising the visit, as was required of them by the Prison Regulations,
expressing his annoyance that Andrea should have mentioned the
matter and taken for granted that the Governors would agree.

A subsequent request was received from Wolf-Rüdiger's family to include their youngest daughter in the visit, since otherwise
she would feel left out of things. In our discussions the Governors
approved the idea of a family visit. However, we were not prepared
to allow the visit to go unsupervised or in any other way to be in
breach of the Prison Regulations, by which the Soviet Governor, in
particular, was bound. One aspect that especially concerned us was
that the prisoner should not be subjected to too emotional an upset
from the impact of seeing these young children. As an elementary
precaution the Medical Orderly would be placed on immediate stand-by. Eventually it was agreed that the duration of the visit
would be limited to one hour, during which any one adult and any
one child could be present in the Visiting Room under the normal
conditions. To facilitate this, the Chief Warders' Office would be put
at the family's disposal, and refreshments provided for the children
waiting their turn to see their grandfather.

However, these terms did not meet the family expectations, so at the last minute Wolf announced that he proposed coming alone. When he arrived he asked permission to shake his father's hand and was refused; throughout the visit he kept clearing his throat nervously. His father appeared to be in excellent health and spirits. He asked why the children had not come and his son explained the reason, to which Hess nodded in assent. Wolf-Rüdiger posed a lot of questions about his father's conditions, including the lift, clearly briefing himself for his forthcoming encounter with the media waiting outside the prison grounds, where special additional security measures had been mounted by the Berlin Police. Arrangements had also been made for the receipt of flowers brought in by the public, these being passed on to the local hospital in due course as they could not be given to the prisoner. The atmosphere between the Governors and Wolf-Rüdiger was sufficiently hostile for the former to avoid shaking his hand when he left, escorted by the American Chief Warder. Darold Keane stated that in view of the way they had chosen to comment on him publicly, he would no longer attend visits by either Wolf Rüdiger or his wife.

At our weekly meeting immediately after this visit, Chernykh again raised the proposal of taking appropriate action against Wolf-Rüdiger for his revelations to the media, as had occurred on several occasions in the past, but it was agreed that we should wait until our next meeting to see the outcome of that day's events. Darold then produced a magnificent cake for our inspection, which had been specially baked for Hess's ninetieth birthday with our prior permission.

On the next visit, in May, Andrea suddenly produced a copy of her husband's newly released book, *Mein Vater Rudolf Hess*, from her handbag and tried to hand it over to her father-in-law. She looked round reproachfully at us when we told her to put it back.

Wolf-Rüdiger had been only three years old when his father flew off to Scotland, and thirty-one when he saw him again. As previously mentioned, Hess did not request the first visit from his family until December 1969, when he suddenly decided to ask his wife and son to come to see him at the BMH. After this first thirty-minute encounter they both emerged visibly shocked, and from that point on Wolf-Rüdiger seems to have taken it on himself to mount a crusade for the release and exoneration of his father.

Early in 1970 he flew to London, where he received much sympathy from such august figures as the late Airey Neave, MP, and the late George Thompson, MP, the then Minister for European Affairs. Upon return to Germany he contacted Dr Alfred Seidl, the lawyer who had defended Hess at Nuremberg and who had later visited him at Spandau on official family business in 1954, 1964, 1966, 1967 and 1969. From this time on their names were linked in the release campaign, founding the '*Freiheit für Rudolf Hess*' Society, which published pamphlets, posters and stickers, and held public meetings in this cause.

To my mind, no one summed up Wolf-Rüdiger's attitude more neatly than *The Times* columnist, Bernard Levin, who had written a series of articles over the years appealing for the release of Rudolf Hess, for instance 'The world is full of prisons' (24 December 1969), 'My plan to bring mercy to Rudolf Hess' (23 December 1971), and 'This enfeebled old man has paid the price' (1 March 1977). However, the release of Wolf-Rüdiger's first book prompted Levin to write a most scathing article, 'The saint of Spandau', from which I quote with his kind permission:

Hess's wife was one of the first women to join the Nazi Party; his son was only three years old at the time of Hess's dramatic solo flight to Britain, in 1941. Both have worked for many years for the ending of Hess's imprisonment in Spandau; I entirely agree that, on compassionate grounds (and on those alone), he should be released, and wrote several articles saying so as long ago as 1969. But I have to say that, having read the son's plea on behalf of the father, I am of the opinion that the objective, which is to enable Hess to end his days with his family in freedom, can only be set back by this shameless and disgusting book.

For it is not the principal contention of Wolf Hess that his father has suffered enough punishment and should suffer no more; he does say that, in places most eloquently, but he says very much more. His book is a demand not that we should pity Hess, but that we should admire him almost without reserve. 'Many striking virtues are combined in my father,' says Wolf Hess, 'will-power, enterprise, sincerity, resolution and honesty towards himself and his ideals.' He is undergoing 'martyrdom' because his 'good intentions were exploited,' though 'there is no cause to petition for mercy, since this implies a recognition of guilt,' and 'there can be no question at all of this.'

How, then, does such a paragon come to be imprisoned at all? It is, broadly speaking, everybody's fault but his own. The peace terms he offered when he flew to Britain would have left Hitler in control of Europe, but Churchill should have accepted them. Roosevelt, longing for the United States to get into the war, would not persuade him to do so. Stalin was incited to stand up to Hitler, who would never have attacked the Soviet Union hadn't it been for Churchill, who was guilty of 'one of the most shameful misdeeds in world history' in his 'sinister attempt to stir up Stalin against Hitler.'

In 1974, Seidl asked to see Hess in order to get him to sign a Power of Attorney that would enable Seidl to take proceedings against the German publishers of Eugene Bird's book. This request was refused as it did not come from the prisoner, and a subsequent request from Hess to see Seidl was also turned down.

Then, in 1975, Seidl had to give up his role as Hess's lawyer when he was appointed Minister of the Interior for Bavaria. An attempt was made to have a Dr Bucher appointed in his stead, but the Russians would not accept this. In July of the same year Rechtsanwalt Engelhardt wrote to the Governors saying that he was representing Hess in his case before the European Commission for Human Rights, and asking for a visit. Hess knew nothing of the matter and the request was denied.

Over the years numerous appeals for release were made by Hess, his son, Seidl, and others. A summary made from FCO records shows that there were a total of twenty-seven Allied appeals to the Soviet authorities, and that the British government participated in all but three of them. The United Kingdom was alone among the Western Allies in appealing at Ministerial level, and did so routinely from 1970 on thirteen separate occasions.

There was a spate of such appeals around the time of Hess's ninetieth birthday in April 1984, including one from the prisoner himself, who had misinterpreted what an American oculist had told him and believed that he would shortly go blind. It took a lot of persuading – not as a counter to his appeal, but as a reassurance for his morale that he was mistaken.

Dr Seidl's appeals were naturally on legal grounds. He produced lengthy arguments to prove the illegality of the Nuremberg sentence and the subsequent detention but these all foundered. As late as October 1976 the European Commission on Human Rights dismissed a case brought by him against the United Kingdom on Hess's behalf.

In May 1983 Seidl became very excited over *Stern* magazine's publication of the so-called 'Hitler Diaries', and sent a spate of letters to the prison asking to interview Hess on this subject. In particular he wanted to pose two specific questions, concerning firstly the keeping of diaries by Hitler, and secondly, whether Hitler had been party to Hess's flight to Britain in 1941. Naturally these requests were ignored. The 'Hitler Diaries' turned out to be an elaborate fraud.

Wolf-Rüdiger Hess's appeals for his father's release all carried their own self-destruct mechanism, beginning with the phrase, '*Mein Vater, ehemahliger Stellvertreter des Führers und Reichsminister. . .*' ('my father, former Deputy to the Führer and Reichsminister. . .') which was guaranteed to irritate, if not prejudice, any recipient.

The standard Soviet response to all appeals was to the effect that the Soviet Union had no grounds for Hess's release. Hess had been a ringleader in the Nazi Reich and one of Hitler's closest lieutenants. To the Soviet people his name was associated with war crimes and the death of over 20 million Soviet citizens. To pardon such a criminal, a hardened defender of Nazism, would be taken as a sign of appeasement by those who still had not learned the harsh lessons of history. Hess was a symbol of Nazi evil. His release would not be understood by the Soviet people, or by other peoples who had suffered from Nazi oppression.

In May 1986 Hess appealed to the four heads of state, American, British, French and Soviet, through the Governors for his release or, failing that, for a month's leave. This was passed on as usual but nothing more was heard of it.

By tradition, the prison chaplain was French, usually from Alsace and fluent in German, being the Protestant padre serving the French garrison in Berlin. The first of my acquaintance was Pasteur Charles Gabel, who had been nine years in the job when, in August 1986, he was dismissed following the discovery of evidence that he had been smuggling items out of the prison for the prisoner, and acting as an intermediary between Hess and his family. He later admitted in his book *Conversations Interdites avec Rudolf Hess* that he had smuggled out Hess's will, which expressed his wish to be buried alongside his parents and brother in the family grave at Wunsiedel, and naming Wolf-Rüdiger, Dr Seidl and Pasteur Gabel as his executors. However, Gabel denied having smuggled out anything else of significance, which was just as well because the subsequent search by Chernykh uncovered a seventeen-page 'testament' by the prisoner on the reasons for the Second World War, and another fifteen pages on more mundane matters.

Significantly, as it would later turn out, Pasteur Gabel wrote of Hess: 'He was bright, even at 92, but what he feared most was failing mentally with age. He could not accept the tumble into senility.'

Pasteur Gabel's replacement was a Pasteur Michel Roehrig, who claimed to have found Christianity at the age of forty, and had then trained for the ministry. Upon arrival at the prison he was briefed by the Board as to the revised regulations applicable to his role, which he promptly breached by showing a Bible to the prisoner, on a blank page of which was a message from Gabel. When reproached he simply pointed upwards and said that he took his orders from above! It was only when Michel Planet was able to assure the Board that Pasteur Roehrig had been severely reprimanded by the French Commandant for this act that he was allowed to continue in this office.

# VII

# Developments and Surprises

In October 1982 an agreement was reached by the Board of Governors with the family, following an appeal in May of that year from Ilse Hess that in the event of Rudolf Hess's death in captivity the body would be handed over to the family for burial. This was a considerable advance on the original Four Power concept of cremation and scattering the ashes to the four winds.

Wolf-Rüdiger signed an agreement to the effect that the burial would take place in Bavaria, discreetly and within the closest family circle. This was countersigned by the Governors four days later, but no copy was given to Wolf-Rüdiger since they mistrusted his possible use of such a document.

The signing of this document, following fast on the signing of the so-called 'Spandau Protocol' of 1 October 1982 by the Berlin Ministers of the Four Powers, cleared the way for the Governors to start work on a paper giving their proposals as to how the eventual closing down of the administration should take place.

I presented the first draft of the 'Governors' Recommendations' paper to the Board on 10 February 1983, but it was not until 29 June that a final text was agreed and signed by the Governors for presentation to their respective Ministers. This paper, however, triggered

off a dispute with the Soviet Embassy about the inclusion of the
standard form of address of the prison as 'Berlin, Germany,' which
they wanted changed to 'Wilhelmstrasse 23, Westberlin [*sic*],' a neat
political point, but one countered in debate by an even neater point
from the American Legal Adviser, as Acting US Governor, with a
reference to the Soviets' own use of the title 'Group of Soviet Forces
in Germany.' The Western Governors stuck to their 'no change'
guns and, eventually in mid-April of the following year, the Soviet
Governor agreed to the removal of the subject from the agenda when
the Ministers of the Four Powers resident in Berlin signed a 'Record
of Meeting' approving the 'Governors' Recommendations.'

The first practical move towards closing down the prison was the
clearance of all the rubbish from the old classrooms on the first floor
of the Administration Block. I organised the loan of a couple of 10-ton
trucks and a platoon from the 2nd Battalion, The Royal Irish Rangers,
to come and clear the area shortly before 5 November. Everything
had to be manhandled down the big spiral stone staircase and through
a wide door out into the yard next to the derelict cookhouse. Two
loads of wood went off to the Maifeld for the garrison Guy Fawkes
Night bonfire, and two loads of scrap metal went to the Ordnance
Services for disposal. Bits of uniform, mattresses and the like we
destroyed on our own bonfire in the yard, adding the two coffins from
the cellar. During the clear-out we came across a metal trunk full of
keys and metal tags related to the prison, and a large flat wooden box
containing an absolute treasure trove of old architects' drawings for
the construction of the prison. These two containers we put into the
Archives for safekeeping.

My next job was to sort out the archives themselves and, with the
aid of the Soviet Governor and his interpreter, to make an inventory
of their contents. Although I had carried out a preliminary survey
on BMG instructions in 1982 with a view to making an estimate of
how much work would be involved in microfilming the records, and
had brought them into some sort of order, a considerable amount of

work still remained to be done. We now had to go through the individual files, weeding out the superfluous carbon copies stemming from pre-photocopier days, and finally ensuring that we had complete sets of minutes and the like, together with their translations.

One aspect of the new planning and agreements had to do with the post-mortem procedures to be carried out once Hess was dead. The original agreement signed by the Governors on 24 March 1955 foresaw the autopsy being performed in the prison's operating theatre either by a pathologist of the nation of the month, or by a readily available pathologist from one of the other three nations. The new arrangements changed the venue to the BMH, and thus in effect placed the onus on the British to provide a prominent pathologist who would operate on behalf of the other nations and in the presence of their observers.

British Sector Headquarters then drew up contingency plans for the provision of a pathologist and the subsequent movement of the body to Bavaria for hand-over to the family. Since it was anticipated that the Special Investigation Branch (SIB) of the Royal Military Police would provide the necessary support for the autopsy as part of an investigation into the circumstances of the death on behalf of the Board, they were tasked with making their own contingency plans, with my assistance. These plans were then practised from time to time with the aid of an Army pathologist flown out for the purpose.

However, we were still dealing with a live – and ageing – prisoner. One of my main tasks was to improve the emergency medical procedures, a process that advanced painfully slowly over the period of my governorship. As early as November 1982 I had managed to introduce my 'Paradox' scheme. The idea behind this was that if the Duty Chief Warder had reason to believe that the prisoner needed urgent medical attention, he could telephone the BMH using 'Paradox' as a code-word that would be understood irrespective of nationality, and a doctor and ambulance would be despatched to the prison without delay. Simultaneously, the Main Gate Warder would telephone the Governors, who would be responsible for summoning their own Medical Advisers. The Duty Chief Warder would open a sealed envelope containing a pass with the names of the duty doctors for that month, so that the Main Gate Warder could admit the doctor and his ambulance immediately upon arrival. This scheme was still severely limited, however, by the fact that all four Medical Advisers had to recommend hospitalisation (if it was found to be necessary), and then the Governors' consent had to be obtained before the prisoner could be moved.

In December 1986 Darold Keane suggested that, in order to speed up the process, the first doctor on the scene should be authorised to make the decision on hospitalisation on his own. Within a month the Soviets had given their approval, and so we were able to work out a greatly improved version of 'Paradox', which included the use of walkie-talkies between the warders on duty and a bleeper system for summoning the Governors, Potsdam, where our Soviet colleague lived, being well within the orbit of our transmitters situated in West Berlin. The walkie-talkies turned out not to work within the prison grounds, but now, with both bleeper and telephone available for alerting the Governors and Medical Advisers, I was able to produce a scheme that reduced the time between the Duty Chief Warder's decision to call for help and the prisoner's entry into the BMH to about thirty minutes, and this came into effect on 1 April 1987.

Meanwhile, the Board had received some nasty shocks. On 25 August 1986, just as the American Sector Commandant was about to make his monthly inspection, the American Chief Warder informed us that some of the items of Hess's uniform, worn on his flight to the United Kingdom in 1941, and since then stored in the first cell on the left inside the Cell Block, were missing. It was decided not to tell the American Sector Commandant during his visit as some preliminary investigation of the circumstances was needed beforehand.

The keys to this cell were not on the Duty Chief Warder's master ring, but kept in the Secretariat and only drawn for visits or when disused items of clothing were to be stored there. It transpired that the leather flying-helmet, which was usually on a small table below the cell window, was missing, as were the Luftwaffe uniform jacket with its captain's insignia, and the forage cap and shoes, all of which had been stored in a cupboard. The bulky leather flying-suit, fur-lined flying boots and the uniform breeches were still there.

Enquiries revealed that the last time the Governors had seen these items had been during the new British Sector Commandant's first inspection in January that year. One of the Soviet warders had drawn the keys and seen the boots and helmet on 27 May, and had again seen the helmet through the spy hole in the door on 17 August, indicating that the theft had taken place during the previous week.

It was then found that the controlling keys could easily be fished out of the letterbox-type opening of the wall safe in which they were placed at night. This system was changed, therefore, and the remaining uniform items transferred to the Archives, to which only the four Governors held keys. The other items from the clothing cell, which had been nominated for destruction in the 1983 'Recommendations,' were then burnt.

However, our embarrassment was not yet complete. In opening the Governors' safe, in which were kept the prison seal for embossing passes and a sealed envelope containing Hess's personal items that had been removed from him in 1947, we found that this envelope had also been emptied. The last occasion on which the contents had been checked was when Chernykh had taken over as Soviet Governor, and I had seen them once before that at some time after I took over. The items missing included Hess's signet ring, a cigarette case that he had presumably used for carrying some of his pills, and two watches, one on a long leather strap which was worn round the thigh when flying as a chronometer check.

The Berlin detachment of the SIB were called in to investigate, assisted by the French and American authorities, but apart from making security recommendations for the Governors to act on, they were unable to trace the culprit. The thief could have been a warder from any of the four nations. With three out of the four nations on duty each day, providing three warders each for the eight-hour shifts and with national sensibilities involved, the pursuit of the investigation proved to be a highly delicate matter. Fortunately, we managed to keep the scandal to ourselves for a while. Clive Freeman eventually got hold of the story and published it in the *Sunday Times* on 12 April 1987, but it did not seem to attract much attention elsewhere. The fact that a British warder had been responsible did not emerge until the following year, as I will relate later.

Another – and recurring – problem that arose in connection with the warders was caused by the photographs of the prisoner periodically published in various magazines. Eugene Bird had been a major culprit in this respect in his time, even taking home-movie films of the prisoner in his environment. Pasteur Gabel, too, had a photograph of Hess standing next to an open Bible. The fact that one or more warders must be involved in this business was greatly disturbing, and led to many a heated discussion by the Board on breaches of prison security, all emphasising the difficulty of ensuring rigid compliance.

Soldiers occasionally managed to smuggle cameras in and take shots from Tower No. 3, although they were all supposed to be searched for such items before going on duty. The only official photography allowed was at the hand-over ceremonies, when one photographer from each of the two nations involved was normally issued a gate pass upon request.

A second major shock came soon afterwards in the early hours of Thursday, 2 October 1986, when I received a telephone call from the RMP Duty Room at British Sector Headquarters informing me that an explosion had just occurred at the prison. I immediately dressed and drove there quickly through the deserted streets from my home in the Westend area of Charlottenburg.

Gatower Strasse opposite the Governors' Mess had been blocked off by the Berlin Police, and had glass and debris strewn right across it. The Mess building itself looked devastated, with smashed windows, curtains hanging out, and cracked walls. The Berlin Fire Brigade were in attendance and had just put out a fire in the room between the Governors' and warders' dining-rooms. Because of the possibility of there being a second explosive device in the building it was decided to leave further investigation until daylight, and the families in House No. 22 were evacuated to accommodation next door in Smuts Barracks for the rest of the night. Again, it was agreed among the Governors that the SIB should be tasked to investigate the explosion in co-operation with the Berlin Police, as the circumstances indicated an outside agency being involved in the crime. At 7am a US Military Police sniffer dog was used to check the building for more explosives before the forensic experts from the SIB and Berlin *Kriminalpolizei (Kripo)* had a look around. Massive structural damage had been caused around the seat of the explosion in the Governors' dining-room, as well as in the rooms adjoining and above. It seemed as if the explosion had been caused by a 'Molotov cocktail' thrown through the corner window. The *Kripo* were left to continue the investigation. Next day, Friday, the SIB returned and recovered several items inside and out that had been overlooked by the *Kripo*, so the SIB captain contacted his *Kripo* colleague and invited him to assist with a more detailed examination of the scene on the Saturday.

On this occasion the debris was carefully sifted and cleared away down to the remains of the carpet, revealing much important evidence. Two prepared fuses of French manufacture were found, one attached to the remains of a wine bottle that had been used as a Molotov cocktail. Examination of the carpet showed that the building had been entered and prepared for burning beforehand. Several large pieces of sponge had been hacked out of the chair squabs and soaked in petrol, as had strips torn from a tablecloth, and from these three separate seats of fire had been prepared. It now appeared that the fumes from these positions had formed a gas cloud in the interval between preparation and ignition, thus reacting something like a domestic gas explosion, although the old plaster ceiling had collapsed and smothered the fire in a cloud of dust before it could take hold.

The odd thing about this whole investigation was that the *Kripo's* forensic experts had done such a poor job on the first day, and then the forensic evidence discovered through SIB persistence was to lose all its labels in the *Kripo* laboratories while awaiting examination. Further, the photographs taken by the *Kripo* allegedly showing where individual items of evidence had been found in the debris used items other than the originals, and were also so badly presented that they would never have stood up in a British court of law. Fortunately, the SIB had recorded the findings properly on film and had their own records of this evidence.

Although these investigations failed to trace the culprits, various unlikely organisations claimed responsibility. The Axel Springer Verlag, the newspaper and magazine publishing conglomerate, had in fact received a letter on 6 October, posted in Berlin, from the '*Sprengkommando Weisse Wolke*' ('White Cloud Explosives Commando'), threatening a bombing attack on the prison if Hess was not released by the 24th of that month. Nobody had heard of such an organisation, nor was this threat taken seriously, being one of many bomb threats received daily in Berlin over one subject or another. Then, on the morning of the explosion, the *Deutsche Presse Agentur* received a telephone call from someone claiming responsibility in the name of the '*Befreiungskommando Rudolf Hess*' ('Hess Liberation Commando').

Nothing further was heard until February 1989, when the Berlin Police arrested a German national for attempted aggravated robbery. Under interrogation, he said that he had been a member of the

'*Sozialpatriotische Aktionsfront*,' which he claimed had been responsible for the attack on the prison Mess. He named two Frenchmen, both fervent admirers of Hess, as being the actual perpetrators, which might explain the French fuses found.

In fact, however, this was not the first occasion that I had had experience of explosives in that building. Just before Christmas 1981 I was told by our Public Safety Branch that one of the Mess cooks at the prison, a German national by the name of Nikola Aljinovic, had been arrested on suspicion of terrorism and had confessed to having stored explosives in the Mess attic. I briefed the other Governors and obtained their permission for the SIB to go into the building and search on behalf of the *Kripo*. It was at some time in the afternoon that we went up the back stairs of the building to search. The little room near the top of the stairs used by Aljinovic for changing contained a wooden locker, in which some clothing was neatly stacked with a beer bottle balanced on top, as if prepared for inspection. Then we went up to the attic and looked around for a considerable time, but could find nothing.

I flew out on leave next day. In my absence the SIB returned with more precise directions, and eventually found the explosive and sixteen detonators hidden in a black plastic bag taped behind a rafter where the roof overhung the outside walls. Aljinovic, despite his German nationality, had been born in Split of Yugoslav parents, and was eventually convicted and received a sentence of two and a half years' imprisonment for his activities as a member of the Croatian Revolutionary Movement, which allegedly had been responsible for the deaths of fourteen people throughout Germany during the previous ten years in an underground struggle with secret agents of the Yugoslav government.

Nevertheless, he was an excellent cook, and I was amused to receive a cutting of an article in the *Bild Zeitung* of 3 February 1988 in which he was said by then to be working in a Berlin restaurant; he also claimed that he had cooked for Hess for six years! As a German employee, of course, he would not have been allowed within the prison walls.

The explosion in House No. 21 had rendered it both uninhabitable and unsafe. Fortunately House No. 24 was empty and, despite years of neglect, proved readily convertible as the new Mess building. While the Public Services Agency made a lightning job of conversion, the Governors and staff fed off the prisoner's kitchen in the Chief Warders' Office, an improvisation that worked quite well, although it put a temporary stop to entertaining visitors.

# VIII

# The Last Lap

In 1987 Berlin celebrated its 750th anniversary on both sides of the Wall in considerable style, making it a very busy and interesting year for all of us in the city. There were visits from many heads of state, including Presidents Reagan and Mitterrand, and Her Majesty the Queen took the salute at her own Birthday Parade on the Maifeld. One way and another the Protocol Officers were kept very much on their toes.

However, life at the prison was not without its own excitements, if on a less elaborately planned basis. At the very beginning of the year Hess became concerned about his pulse rate. Having heard of the successful result of an operation to insert a pacemaker in his son's father-in-law (who happened to be twenty years younger), he made a formal request for the insertion of a pacemaker under a general anaesthetic. As a result of this he was monitored by a cardiograph for twenty-four hours, which failed to reveal any irregularity that would warrant such an operation. When Wolf-Rüdiger Hess visited the prison, the Medical Advisers explained the situation to him. He was not satisfied with this, however, wanting a German specialist to examine his father, and even writing a letter to Chancellor Kohl asking him to intervene on his father's behalf. Sending a copy of this letter to the Governors, he asked that he be sent a copy of the cardiograph read-out, but this request was rejected.

Instead, it was decided to fly in a specialist from St Thomas's Hospital in London to examine Hess. This gentleman confirmed the previous findings that the insertion of a pacemaker, except in an emergency, was unnecessary, but he did suggest a change in the medicaments being provided, which was promptly adopted.

Then, at 4am on the morning of 1 March, Hess was admitted to the BMH with what was diagnosed as pneumonia. Naturally this involved a full turn-out of Medical Advisers and Governors in the middle of the night, as well as all those involved in the convoy and security arrangements.

An entire floor of the multi-storey BMH building was permanently reserved for the hospitalisation of Hess. Security was intense. A platoon of infantry guarded the hospital, imposing identity checks at the entrance gate, at the lift, and at the lift exit on the prison floor. Down the corridor there was then an RMP close-security check before one came to the area guarded by two of the prison warders. The two-bed ward used for Hess was equipped with a ceiling-high mesh screen for security purposes just short of the window, but otherwise was of the same high standard as the rest of the BMH facilities.

One of the hospital's four lifts had an override device, used when Hess was present, whereby the lift only travelled between the ground floor, where the operating theatres were located, and his own special floor. However, on one memorable occasion this device had not yet been activated when Hess was loaded into the lift with his medical attendants. The Governors decided to use the stairs and were surprised to arrive before the prisoner, who had meantime made an unexpected trip to the Quartermaster's Department in the basement.

At about 8am on the morning of 6 March Wolf-Rüdiger telephoned me at home to ask how his father was and to ask for permission to visit him on the 11th. On my way to the office I called in at the BMH and spoke with the doctor tending Hess. He reported the pneumonia almost cured, but that signs of the approach of senility had been observed in the prisoner's behaviour. He said he was conducting tests of the treatment being given to ensure that it was not having an adverse effect on Hess's mental processes.

After consulting with the CO of the BMH about the implications of this new factor, I convened an emergency meeting of the Board to discuss this news, as senility was an aspect we had not hitherto contemplated. If the old man was to become senile we would have to provide twenty-four hour nursing cover, involving the recruitment of a further four medical orderlies. It was decided to ask the British Labour Office to advertise the four posts as if for employment at the BMH. Wolf-Rüdiger's request to visit on the 11th was also agreed, and I was to inform him by telephone that his father was staying on in hospital for recuperation after the completion of the course of treatment for his pneumonia.

Wolf-Rüdiger telephoned me again on the morning of the 10th asking to defer his visit until the 12th, but I was now obliged to tell him that his father, having been informed of the proposed visit on the 11th, had insisted that the visit did not take place until the last day of the month. Wolf-Rüdiger said that he would come anyway.

We held another extraordinary meeting on the 11th to discuss this visit. We felt certain that Wolf-Rüdiger would hold a press conference, so we decided to clarify with the prisoner his refusal to see his son until the end of the month, and have him put it in writing, which he did. Hess remained adamant. He did not want his son to see him in his present state. We therefore decided to allow Wolf-Rüdiger to question the physician treating his father about his state of health.

When Wolf-Rüdiger turned up at the BMH on the 12th he was accompanied by his lawyer, Dr Seidl. A bevy of journalists and photographers were waiting outside the hospital. Seidl's request also to see the prisoner was denied outright. Wolf-Rüdiger was shown his father's note but refused to accept it as genuine, (it was undated). He persisted in his demand to see his father and we were unable to persuade him otherwise, so eventually, out of sympathy for his case, we decided upon 'seeing is believing' and gave him the loan of an office to write out a formal application to visit, which was then promptly granted on the understanding that he was only to see his father and not approach him without the latter's consent, bearing in mind his father's resolute refusal.

We escorted him upstairs to the prisoner's ward, where we went into the outer area of the room in which his father was sitting, propped up on two chairs and covered with a blanket. Michel Planet approached Hess and told him that he had a surprise for him – his son had come to see him. Hess said emphatically that he did not want to see his son now, not until the last day of the month. Wolf-Rüdiger could not contain himself and cried out words to the effect: 'Father, it's me, your son! I have come to talk to you. Don't you recognise me?' Hess gave no sign of recognition, but simply repeated his previous statement. There was nothing else to do but withdraw in embarrassment. Wolf-Rüdiger looked as if he was in a state of shock. What he had failed to realise was that the old man's pride simply would not allow him to be seen by his son in such a weak and feeble condition.

As expected, Wolf immediately gave a press conference outside the hospital, during which, much to the annoyance of the Board, he revealed the existence of the confidential agreement of October 1982 concerning the hand-over of the body to the family for burial. However, it was felt that any punitive measures taken against him, such as denial of visits, would be more to the detriment of the prisoner than himself.

On Saturday 14 March a meeting was held to discuss the return of Hess to the prison. The French Medical Adviser opposed the motion, however, and so it was not until the Monday that unanimous agreement was reached and the prisoner returned, by which time the indications of the approach of senility had virtually disappeared. This was just as well, for we had had no success as yet in our recruiting campaign, and the BMH was stretched to provide the male nurses needed to keep an eye on Hess when Melaouhi was off duty.

Eventually only one suitable applicant, a Jamaican woman, appeared, and she not until mid April. I went to the British Labour Office in a staff car to pick her up and explained to her on the way to the prison what the job was that we were offering. She seemed both intelligent and happy to take the job on. The question of females in the Cell Block was now no longer an obstacle, and the Board agreed to take her on probation.

However, earlier that month Hess had raised an objection with Darold Keane about a black American warder, Jordan, claiming that the latter was unsympathetic and discourteous and that Jordan's very presence was causing him heart palpitations. Quite rightly Darold dismissed this claim as absurd; Jordan was well known and liked among the rest of us at the prison for his quiet, courteous conduct. Hess had then repeated his complaint to the American Commandant during the monthly inspection. Jordan was then temporarily kept out of the Cell Block on Main Gate duty as a precautionary measure while the complaint was considered, but a firm rejection of Hess's plea duly came back from the US Mission and Jordan was duly reinstated in his normal duties, including escorting the prisoner.

Now Hess's colour prejudice showed again, with him doing everything possible to avoid the new nurse, including getting up at 5am to take his bath unescorted. By the end of the first week of her employment he was readmitted to the BMH with heart palpitations and we were obliged to dismiss her, despite our reluctance to yield to his racism.

This colour prejudice had first shown itself when Melaouhi took over as Medical Orderly. As previously related, however, Melaouhi, whose skin colouring in any case was very light, had proved himself to the prisoner with his gentle ministrations in very little time, and had won his confidence.

The reason for the palpitations, however, related to something entirely different. Hess had been experimenting with his diet in an attempt to combat the bouts of incontinence he was now experiencing, and his palpitations had occurred after he had eaten three hard-boiled eggs in rapid succession.

This second spell in the BMH had only lasted twenty-four hours and the medical reports from that time give no indication that Hess was suffering from incontinence, other than some problem with the control of his bladder. It seems, however, that his own sense of pride led him to conceal this from the Medical Advisers as being too shameful. I recall seeing him with wads of cotton wool stuffed down his trousers for the first time when I returned from leave in late July of 1987.

In fact the medical reports consistently showed him to be in good condition for his age, and it was a standing joke among the Medical Advisers that he would fulfil the aim he had expressed on his ninetieth birthday that he would live to see his hundredth.

A significant event – again, in the light of what happened later – took place during my absence on leave that summer. Hess asked to see a copy of the Nuremberg judgement on him. This was approved by the Board on 17 July and the papers were passed to him, exactly one month before his death.

# IX

# Death in the Afternoon

On the afternoon of 17 August 1987 I had an appointment with Dr Anatoly Jashin, my Soviet protocol counterpart, at 3pm at the Soviet Embassy on the Unter den Linden, in this case a low-level reply to a previously delivered Soviet protest. Consequently it was not until about 4pm that I got back to the office at British Sector Headquarters, where my secretary told me that I was wanted urgently at the prison. On my way out I encountered the Political Adviser, who informed me that Hess was probably dead and advised me to get to the hospital as soon as possible.

What had happened that fateful afternoon I have reconstructed from the individual statements contained in the SIB report on the investigation. The British already had contingency plans for the SIB to investigate the circumstances of Hess's death whenever and wherever it occurred, including covering the autopsy, and also to record for posterity the environment in which Hess had lived as a counter to any accusations of needless cruelty or neglect that might arise later. It so happened that on that afternoon a team under an experienced SIB major (I had known him as an SIB sergeant years before) was conducting an investigation in Brooke Barracks, next door to the prison, so they were ready to hand. It appears that as soon as it had been established that Hess was dead, they were tasked by the British Sector Headquarters Chief of Staff and were able to start their investigation straight away, although the Board of Governors were neither aware of this nor asked to give their approval until later in the day.

August being an American month, the guard on duty was provided by the 5th Battalion, 502nd Infantry Regiment. There were no Soviet staff on duty, the Main Gate Warder being British, the Duty Chief Warder French, and the warder in attendance on the prisoner the black American, Jordan.

When Jordan took over responsibility for the prisoner in the Cell Block at about noon he found Hess to be in a very good mood, seemingly quite cheerful. Shortly after 1.30pm Hess asked permission to go into the garden and started getting ready. Normally he would have taken anything from forty-five minutes to an hour to prepare himself for his outing, but on this occasion he was a lot quicker and they entered the lift together at about 2.10pm. When the lift reached ground level Jordan went ahead to unlock the lift compound door and the Portakabin, while Hess followed on at his own pace, wearing a long raincoat over his indoor clothing and a straw sombrero.

The guard commander doing his round of the sentries passed between them at this juncture. He saw Jordan waiting outside the Portakabin and Hess walking slowly through the garden. The sentry in Tower No. 3, who had never seen Hess before, watched him make his way down the path, stopping frequently to look around. It seems that he must have been taking farewell of his beloved garden.

When he reached the Portakabin, Hess went inside and closed the door behind him. After removing his outer garments he then appears to have stood with his back to the wall between the door and little window, where a 2.75-metre long white plastic-coated electrical extension cable was firmly knotted to the window handle at the female socket end, 1.40 metres from the floor. This cable was used with one of the four reading lamps provided there for him to read by, and had long been knotted in position. A sergeant of the guard later confirmed that he had seen it there when he started duty at the prison at the beginning of the month.

Hess then apparently looped the loose end of the cable round his neck and tied it there with a simple once-over slip knot. He then slid his back down the wall with his legs sticking out in front of him. This movement caused the knot to tighten and at the same time to slide some distance down the length of the cable, so providing a constantly tightening loop around his neck, resulting in asphyxiation and heart failure.

When Jordan looked in on a routine check a few minutes later, he found Hess sitting slumped against the wall, the cable stretched taut above him. Jordan later recalled pulling the cable away from Hess's neck and that it came away easily. He could not remember seeing a knot, but it was still there, by then at floor level as a result of Jordan's action, when the SIB photographer recorded the scene.

Hess's mouth and eyes were open, and he appeared to Jordan to be still alive. Jordan quickly placed him on his back with a rolled-up blanket under his head and loosened his clothing, before running off to the rear door of the Cell Block to get to the telephone located on the spiral staircase. He contacted the Main Gate Warder and asked for medical assistance, triggering off the 'Paradox' procedures. He then ran back to the Portakabin, where Hess no longer appeared to him to be breathing.

Meanwhile the guard in Tower No. 3 had been attracted by Jordan's nervous behaviour as he ran to and fro, and had alerted the guardroom by radio. Then Jordan asked him if he could do first aid, but the guard was strictly forbidden to leave his post, so he radioed the guardroom again. This brought the guard commander to investigate. He thought Hess looked dead but detected a weak pulse, so he told the guard in Tower No. 3 to radio the guardroom for medical assistance.

There were two qualified field combat medical orderlies with the guard. The one in charge of the guards' quarters in the barrack block outside the walls received a summons by radio at 2.40pm. He snatched up his first-aid pack and ran to the Main Gate, where the warder was holding the wicket open for him. Inside the court-yard the guard sergeant then led him through the right-hand gate to where Jordan was waiting.

Shortly after this American medical orderly had started examin-ing Hess, Melaouhi arrived and they began the cardio-pulmonary resuscitation process together, while Jordan was sent off to fetch some oxygen. The second American medical orderly then arrived and joined in their attempts to revive the patient.

In response to the 'Paradox' call a British medical officer and an ambulance from the BMH arrived at the prison at 3.12pm and were promptly admitted. The doctor was satisfied with the efforts at resus-citation being carried out by the medical orderlies and Melaouhi. After consulting the CO of the BMH, Colonel John Hamer-Philip, by telephone, the doctor had the Mercedes ambulance driven through the side gate into the grounds as close as possible to the Portakabin, and then had Hess loaded into the ambulance, where they continued their attempts to revive him. The doctor, Melaouhi, the second American medical orderly and Jordan accompanied Hess to the BMH, where they arrived at about 3.50pm. Further attempts at resuscitation were carried out but eventually, at 4.10pm, Colonel Hamer-Philip declared life extinct.

The Governors, Medical Advisers and their interpreters assembled in the prisoner's ward at the BMH. Lieutenant-Colonel Chernykh was on leave in Siberia at the time, so his deputy, Mr Kolodnikov, supported by Senior Lieutenant Dmitri Naumenko and Medical Lieutenant-Colonel Koslikov, eventually arrived from Potsdam. As Chairman, Darold Keane's first task was to notify Wolf-Rüdiger Hess of the death of his father. Even with two telephone operators concentrating on the task, contact was not established until 6.35pm, by which time Wolf-Rüdiger had clearly heard that something was wrong and had tried to contact me at home.

Meanwhile the body had been stripped and given a radiological examination before being stored in the mortuary down in the cellars of the hospital, guarded by two warders.

The contents of the pockets were sealed in an envelope, which Colonel Hamer-Philip gave to Darold Keane.

It was 7.55pm before the Board could formally convene in the room set aside for them in the hospital. Despite a certain atmosphere of finality, climax almost, the meeting was conducted in the usual manner. It began with Colonel Hamer-Philip handing each of the Governors a copy of the Certificate of Death signed by him, which gave the time of death as 4.10pm, with the primary cause as 'cardiac arrest following asphyxia' and the secondary as 'generalised atherosclerosis'–that is, old age. In return he asked us to sign a 'Certificate of Authority for Post-mortem Examination.'

The Board then went on to discuss the content of the press statement concerning Hess's death, which had already been issued by the BMG Information Officer in accordance with the previously mentioned 1982 Ministers' Agreement, but which unfortunately did not cover the contingency of suicide, and therefore no longer met the bill. This statement read:

> Rudolf Hess, one of the major Nazi criminals sentenced in 1946 to life imprisonment by the International Military Tribunal at Nuremberg, died in the Spandau Allied Prison on 17 August 1987. In accordance with a decision of the Four Powers, and after the necessary arrangements have been made, the body of Rudolf Hess will be handed over for burial to the family residing in the Federal Republic of Germany.

There was, as could be expected, intense media interest following the initial announcement of Hess's death, and the Information Officer found himself in the middle of it. BMG, supported by the French and Americans, were anxious to issue a more appropriate statement, but Kolodnikov was under strict instructions to adhere to the letter of the 1972 agreement, a copy of the Russian-language version of which he had with him, and therefore had to request amendments through his ponderous chain of command. Adhering to the Prison Rules, the Western Allies could not act unilaterally in this matter, but the pressure was on and we were constantly having to interrupt our meetings over the next few days to take or make telephone calls from and to our respective superiors, trying to resolve this impasse.

A second statement, issued simultaneously with the first, read:

> The purpose of Spandau Allied Prison has ceased on the death of Rudolf Hess, one of the major Nazi criminals sentenced in 1946 to life imprisonment by the International Military Tribunal at Nuremberg. In accordance with the decision of the representatives of Great Britain, France, the USA and the USSR, the Allied Prison Administration will be permanently terminated. The prison will be demolished.

The general comment, often to be repeated in the succeeding weeks, was 'Thank God, it happened in an American month,' implying that they would have to take the lead. In fact it did not quite turn out like that, firstly because at the higher political levels joint action was necessary between the nations, among whom the British were always the most sensitive to public reaction, and secondly, because the American Governor felt the burden of responsibility in this matter so acutely that his health barely stood up to the strain. This did not go unnoticed by his superiors, and both the American Commandant and their Legal Adviser asked me to help Darold Keane out as much as I could, which of course I did.

The meeting on the evening of the 17th ended with the opening of the sealed envelope containing the contents of Hess's pockets, which included a small alarm clock, four handkerchiefs, two pairs of spectacles, a comb, three pencils, two small marking pens, four ball-point pens, and a letter. This letter proved to be a suicide note, and had been written on the back of the first page of a two-page letter from Andrea Hess, dated 20 July 1987, on the front of which Hess had noted having replied to it on 14 August. The suicide note, as later published by Wolf-Rüdiger, read as follows:

*Bitte an die Direktoren dies heimzuschicken. Geschrieben em paar Minuten vor meinem Tode. Ich danke Euch allen, meine Lieben, für alles was Ihr mir Lieben angetan.*

*Freiburg sagt, es hat mir maßlos Leid getan, daß ich so tun mußte seid dem Nürnberger Prozeß als kenne sie nicht. Es blieb mir nichts anderes übrig, sonst wären alle Versuche unmöglich gewesen in die Freiheit zukommen.*

*Ich hatte mich so darauf gefreut sie wiederzusehen, ich bekam ja Bilder von ihr wie von Euch allen.*

*Euer Großer*

Would the Governors please send this home. Written a few minutes before my death.

I thank you all my loved ones for all that you have done for me.

Tell Freiburg that I was infinitely sorry that I had to behave ever since the Nuremberg Trials as if I did not know her. There remained nothing else for me, otherwise all attempts to free me would have been in vain. I had looked forward to seeing her again. I have received photographs of her as well as of all of you.

Your Big One

The reference to 'Freiburg' was indeed puzzling, and the translation of '*Freiburg sagt*,' initially caused some confusion when it was rendered as 'Freiburg says'. However, a little research revealed that 'Freiburg' was in fact Hess's secretary, Hildegard Fath, who had been greatly distressed when, called as a witness during his trial at Nuremberg, Hess had refused to recognise her. She was one of two of his secretaries, and had been responsible for obtaining secret reports for him about weather conditions over the United Kingdom and the North Sea prior to his flight.

The Board later agreed to the examination of this letter by a handwriting expert as part of the overall investigation into the circumstances of Hess's death, provided that it was conducted within the prison itself in the presence of at least one of the Governors. Consequently a handwriting expert was sent out from the Laboratory of the Government Chemist in London. He appeared equipped with just a briefcase and was sat down in the Governors' room at my desk, which was nearest to the window bay. Before starting his examination, the expert pointed out that he was not operating under laboratory conditions, nor was he familiar with either the German language or the kind of script used by the prisoner. Nevertheless, he was able to establish the authenticity of the note. As a basis for the comparison of Hess's handwriting, I gave him the notebooks recovered from Hess's cell, together with the suicide note and the pens found on the body. These notebooks were later destroyed.

# X

# Two Autopsies, Two Burials

Since the post-mortem arrangements had been previously rehearsed on several occasions by SIB specialist teams under the direction of Lieutenant-Colonel Menzies, a British Army pathologist, the necessary equipment was set up with the minimum of delay. The size of the autopsy room limited the number of people who could be present to the appointed pathologist, Professor J.M. Cameron, the five in the SIB team, and the four national medical observers, of which both the British and American happened to be pathologists themselves. Closed-circuit television enabled the Governors and warders outside to observe what was going on if they so wished. I do not think any of them did! The Acting Soviet Governor had vetoed the idea of taking photographs, so no photographic record could be made.

We assembled at 8am on 19 August, and the whole procedure was over before lunch, with Hess's body neatly sealed in a zinc-lined coffin within a new oak casket and placed in the BMH's Chapel of Rest, still guarded by warders, for the onward journey the next day. We assembled for lunch in the BMH Officers' Mess, by which time Professor Cameron had produced a provisional autopsy report for circulation. This contained a few typing errors which were eventually corrected in the final report that came out several weeks later, following the completion of all the necessary laboratory tests on various specimens removed from the corpse for investigation in the United Kingdom. The cause of death in Professor Cameron's report was given as:

'A. ASPHYXIA, B. COMPRESSION OF THE NECK, C. SUSPENSION.'

Next morning we again assembled early at 7.30am at the BMH for the trip to Grafenwöhr, north-east of Nuremberg, the agreed hand-over point to the Hess family. Senior Lieutenant Dmitri Naumenko, the Soviet interpreter accompanying Kolodnikov, wore civilian clothing for a change. The French Commandant had asked, through Michel Planet, for Pasteur Roehrig to be permitted to accompany us, as he particularly wanted to attend Hess's funeral.

Before leaving, we Governors were each handed a separate copy of the certificate recording the registration of death by the BAOR Registering Officer, who had been specially brought up from HQ BAOR for this purpose. The certificate named me as the informant, 'who saw the dead body,' with the cause of death as 'asphyxia due to compression of the neck due to suspension' as certified by Professor Cameron. It gave the name of the deceased as 'Rudolf Walther Richard Hess,' born '26 April 1894' at 'Alexandria, Egypt.'

Pasteur Roehrig was there, in French Army uniform, briefly holding up progress to say prayers over the coffin as it was removed from the chapel and then placed in the enclosed van for conveyance to RAF Gatow. The RMP-escorted convoy was deployed in the sunken courtyard behind the hospital and, once we had taken our places in the staff cars assigned us, the APM gave the radio signal and off we went. A group of photographers was waiting opposite the hospital entrance, but those waiting outside RAF Gatow were to be bitterly disappointed, for we turned into the emergency gate a hundred metres short of them and drove straight through the complex to emerge on the airfield itself, and then continued on to the transit building. Waiting outside on the tarmac was a Hercules four-engined transport with its loading ramp down. The four assigned warders, one from each nation, took the coffin from the van and walked up the ramp to place it on a stand in the rear of the aircraft, a subject which photographers on the public road running crossways beyond the end of the runway were able to pick up. The crew then drew across some black curtains and closed the rear doors while they took the coffin off the stand and lashed it to the deck for the flight. It was to be the last flight for someone who had once been a most daring pilot.

Coffee and biscuits were served in the VIP lounge while this was going on, and we were politely asked to take the opportunity of using the toilets as those aboard the aircraft were rather primitive. Shortly afterwards we were summoned aboard, where we found that special passenger seats had been installed transversely in the centre of the aircraft for the Governors, the rest of the party having to use the normal canvas seats, ranged along the fuselage sides, designed for parachutists. Earplugs were issued as the engines roared into life and the Hercules moved off.

Just over an hour later, at 10.15am, we landed at Grafenwöhr, a US Army airstrip adjacent to their vast Vogelsang Training Area to the north-east of Nuremberg. The abruptly-applied reverse thrust of the engines as we landed indicated the shortness of the runway and soon we were moving and manoeuvring backwards – the first time I had ever experienced this in an aircraft under its own power. Once the door was opened the loadmaster beckoned and, as previously agreed with Darold Keane, who was obviously not feeling at all well, I went out to reconnoitre the situation.

I saw that we were backed into a confined area between two small corrugated-iron helicopter hangars, one of which, to the rear and right, was open. The runway was about a hundred metres away across the front of the aircraft, with a busy road running parallel to it. Outside the perimeter fence and partially concealed by bushes, I could see a considerable number of cameramen, but they obviously could not see more than the nose and flanks of the aircraft. A US Army major in fatigue uniform, and with no less than two walkie-talkie radios on his belt, was standing at attention immediately behind the aircraft. As I approached him he saluted and introduced himself in drill book fashion as the project officer. I shook his hand and explained to him that, as the Chairman American Governor was rather elderly and not feeling too well, I, as the British Governor, was checking things over for him before anyone left the aircraft. The officer showed me that a table and chairs had been set up in the open hangar for a conference, should that be necessary, and that coffee and telephone and toilet facilities were available in the hut beyond. The area had been taped off, and was guarded by a few military policemen in the charge of a female captain. Satisfied with the arrangements, I went back to get the others from the aircraft, the tail doors of which were then opened.

We hung around waiting for Wolf-Rüdiger Hess to arrive. The sun was shining and it was a pleasant warm day. Eventually, at about 11am, we were informed that Wolf-Rüdiger's car had arrived at the main camp gate with a van and a police escort. I was asked whether they could be admitted. The particulars of the persons concerned had already been passed by me to the US Mission for relay to Grafenwöhr the evening before, but they checked them all over again with me on the spot. It was decided that the police escort could remain at the gate to await the return of the collecting party, since there was no requirement for them within the camp confines.

However, it was another forty minutes or so, with several false alarms on the radio, before Wolf-Rüdiger's Mercedes appeared, closely followed by a plain green van. These vehicles were directed into the open hangar where we had gathered. Wolf-Rüdiger Hess and Dr Seidl got out of the car, followed by Wieland Hess carrying a camera. I immediately called out 'No photography!' and so he put the camera back in the car. We all shook hands, then Darold asked

Wolf-Rüdiger if he was prepared to accept the body of his father, which he said he was. The van was then backed up under the tail of the aircraft and, as we watched from inside the hangar, the coffin was loaded into the van by the four warders. The van's rear doors were closed and it was driven back into the hangar. The security arrangements were such that the photographers on the other side of the airstrip were only able to get pictures of the closed van driving back into the hangar.

Darold then asked Wolf-Rüdiger if he had any questions, and when he said he had none, Darold said: 'Well, I think that concludes our business.' Michel then said that Pasteur Roehrig wished to accompany them with a view to attending the funeral, but Wolf-Rüdiger said he did not know the man. The Pasteur looked taken aback. A final handshake, and they got into the car. It was 12.10pm. I noticed that some of the numerals on the car's number-plate had been obscured with masking tape, and that the van's registration had been completely masked off. As they drove off, Wieland Hess immediately started using his camera, so we directed the major to have them stopped at the perimeter gate and the film confiscated.

We went back to the hut to telephone our people in Berlin to say that the mission had been accomplished, while the Pasteur changed into civilian clothes to make his own way out of the camp. When we came out to board the aircraft, the major was still on his radio, while the Soviets were arguing furiously with the Americans because the latter claimed that they had no authority to confiscate Wieland's film. I managed to persuade them to board the aircraft, saying that it was up to the Americans to sort out the problem and that we would achieve nothing by hanging about any longer.

The aircraft was taxiing to the take-off point when a message came for us to return to the area by the hangars. The major came aboard once more and spoke to Darold, then disappeared. The noise of the engines prevented anyone else hearing what was being said. We stayed for about ten minutes with the engines running before the major returned, spoke to Darold again, and then left. The door closed and we moved off. I approached Darold and asked why we had been held up. He said that first the major had reported that Wieland Hess had gone on taking photographs in the main camp, and then he had come back to say that they had decided they could do nothing about it and it would be better to let them go!

The crew invited Michel and myself to sit on the flight-deck for the return flight, lending us spare headsets so that we could hear what was going on. We sat on the bunk behind the navigator, watching the two pilots, the engineer and the navigator at work. The flight back to Berlin took just eighty minutes, and allowed us some splendid views of the countryside below from time to time. As we came up to the south-western corner of the city we were invited to stand one either side of the pilots, holding on to the seat backs and a grab handle on the canopy. There was a fantastic view of the city as we flew as far as Alexanderplatz to turn near the East Berlin television tower and go all the way back over the Kurfürstendamm, the Grunewald forests and the Havel lakes to Gatow. The pilot was so skilled that I did not even sense the impact of the wheels as we touched down. We returned to the prison for a late lunch, with a sense of relief at having completed this phase successfully. After lunch we held a meeting to record these momentous events.

Meanwhile, Wolf-Rüdiger had taken his father's body to Munich for a second autopsy, which was carried out by the eminent German pathologist, Professor Spann, next day, 21 August. As a check on Professor Cameron's work seeking the cause of death, this second autopsy was somewhat limited in scope by the lack of certain specimens removed during the first autopsy for laboratory analysis in the United Kingdom. What did emerge in the subsequent report, however, was an emphasis, not given in Professor Cameron's report, on the neck markings from the hanging. Presumably, since Professor Spann's knowledge of the case outside his own autopsy findings was limited to the press releases, he found it hard to equate these markings with the hangings of his experience, whereas Professor Cameron had been fully briefed on the SIB findings as they were then known. Consequently Professor Spann's report concluded that death had not been due to natural causes but to strangulation by means of a strong implement, which he did not define further.

Then followed a macabre photograph session with Wolf-Rüdiger and Wieland Hess posing beside the open coffin, the former look-ing distinctly unwell. Copies of one of these photographs were even reproduced in some of the more sensationalist newspapers, and Wolf-Rüdiger was to use three of them in his book on the death of his father two years later.

Next day, Wolf-Rüdiger went to see his mother to discuss the problems of a temporary secret burial, as the local authorities in Wunsiedel, where the family burial plot was located, were unwill-ing to accept the body while there was so much adverse attention focused on their town in the wake of Hess's death. Hess's death had excited the neo-Nazi groups, who were expected to make a mass demonstration at the funeral. The pressures were building up and in the evening of the following day, Sunday 23 August, Wolf-Rüdiger suffered a severe heart attack at home that was to put him out of circulation for the rest of the year.

But the body was still in Munich awaiting burial and now poor Andrea Hess was the only remaining responsible member of the family who could do anything about it. The police, meanwhile, had apparently worked out a solution to the problem, but, if secrecy was to be maintained, the burial had to take place that very night. So, on the same night as her husband's heart attack, Andrea had to identify the body and be photographed next to the open coffin before it could be sealed prior to burial. Then she had to accompany the spe-cial police team to witness the interment.

Where Hess was actually buried remains a Federal state secret, although an article in *Die Actuelle* magazine of 7 November 1987 gave some most interesting, and seemingly authentic, information on the subject. The piece states that the secret operation lasted for the whole of three days between 20 and 23 August, and that only eight Ministry of the Interior officials were involved, all sworn to secrecy. They had to take the corpse from the Institute for Forensic Medicine in Munich and bury it in a pre-selected village graveyard, without anyone in authority in the locality or responsible for the graveyard knowing about it. Firstly they had to find a grave-digger prepared to undertake a technically illegal burial, but here they had some luck, for they found not just one but two individuals willing to do the job.

The operation began with several vans, of the type used for conveying corpses, leaving the Munich Institute in different directions in order to fool the representatives of the media, who were thus obliged to scour the countryside for graveyards with freshly dug graves. The coffin was then put in a normal minibus, as camouflage, and Andrea Hess and the official in charge got in with it. They were then followed by an unmarked car containing the two plain-clothes policemen responsible for the security of the operation.

It was almost midnight when they reached the designated graveyard. The nearest houses were about a hundred yards away. The two waiting grave-diggers opened the cemetery gate to admit the minibus and directed it to where they had already secretly marked out the grave to be dug. The car remained outside with the two policemen keeping watch as the grave-diggers worked by torchlight. Because of the need for haste, and also because it could be expected that at some time in the foreseeable future the body would be removed to a proper burial place, the grave was not dug as deep as the regulations demand. However, great care had to be taken to ensure that they left no evidence of a grave having been dug there.

It was while they were carefully clearing up the site that two incidents occurred which almost ruined the operation. A local resident noticed the car outside the cemetery and informed the local police, who sent a patrol round to investigate. The escorting plain-clothes policemen could not disclose their true identity to the patrol, and were afraid that the others inside the cemetery might finish and give the game away by starting up the minibus. Fortunately they managed to convince the patrol that they had just happened to have stopped there for a rest during the course of a long drive.

Shortly afterwards, a woman suddenly appeared following the tyre-marks up to the cemetery gate. The plain-clothes men only just managed to stop her in time, accosting her in the guise of detectives on the look-out for desecrators. She explained that she was the girl-friend of one of the local grave-diggers, who had gone out to meet someone without telling her who or where, and that she had been unable to sleep for jealousy. Just then the minibus emerged from the cemetery, and when she saw her boyfriend and his colleague she calmed down. The operation was safe.

The article in *Die Actuelle* says (if it is not complete fiction) Hess was temporarily buried in a little cemetery somewhere in south-ern Bavaria. Seven months later, early in the morning of 17 March 1988, Rudolf Hess's body was quietly re-interred in the family plot at Wunsiedel in the presence of Wolf-Rüdiger Hess, his wife Andrea, and their three children. Later a new gravestone was erected with the names of those members of the Hess family previously interred in the plot inscribed on either side of a centrepiece which bore, in more prominent letters, the words:

RUDOLF HESS
26.4.1894–17.8.1987
ICH HAB'S GEWAGT

This unusual epitaph translates roughly as 'I dared' or 'I made a gamble.'

# XI

# Clearing Up

With Hess's body disposed of, it was now time to turn to the tasks involved in the clearing of the prison. Meanwhile the investigation into the prisoner's death was still in progress, and was to be extended until every possible point had been covered to the satisfaction of the governments of the Four Powers.

Lieutenant-Colonel Chernykh returned to duty at the prison on 24 August, somewhat annoyed at having been recalled from his leave in Siberia, only to be stuck in Moscow with insufficient priority to be able to continue his journey until it was too late to take part in the Grafenwöhr trip.

It was decided to maintain the Main Gate Warder's post until such time as we could hand over the prison to the British military authorities. However, the other warders were put on a nine-to-five, five-day week basis as a workforce for clearing the prison, and Melaouhi, the two boilermen, Hess's two cooks, and four other employees were all given notice.

On the night of 24/25 August the Royal Engineers erected a 2-metre tall fence along the Wilhelmstrasse perimeter, enclosing all the external buildings with the main prison in a secure area. A double gate was installed across the entrance and notices put up announcing that the premises were now under the control of the British Commandant. This fencing had been stored next door in Smuts Barracks in anticipation of the event. A Portakabin was set up next to the new gate as a guardroom and manned by a detachment from the duty battalion.

The PSA collaborated in establishing at great speed a secure area on the first floor of House No. 24. Wire mesh was fitted over the windows and a steel door was put in, sealing off the area of the British and French flag rooms. Chernykh was still unhappy over the security of the building itself, so the Royal Engineers set up a Dannert wire fence around it.

Our contact man from *Bauamt Süd* (the local city survey-or's office) confirmed that the *Senator für Justiz* Department did not wish to have any items that they had funded over the years returned to them from the prison, so we were able to proceed on that basis. Darold Keane had the Cell Block cleared by the after-noon of Friday the 28th, and so the Secretariat moved into House No. 24 the following Monday. From this point on, the Governors met for lunch almost every day, Chernykh and Darold because they were fully engaged in the details of the operation, and Michel Planet and myself because we had to keep a close eye on things on behalf of our respective Military Governments. This was also use-ful in enabling the four of us to deal collectively with problems as they arose.

Two large skips were brought into the prison courtyard for the collection of scrap wood and iron, the latter being later taken to be mixed with other scrap at the Ordnance Depot. Trolleys and cardboard boxes were borrowed from the Ordnance Services to help move the archives and other items.

I do not know what there is about having the opportunity to be destructive that excites people so much, but even I put on my jeans and helped throw the old furniture down the stone entrance staircase. A small truck borrowed from the PSA was used to convey most of the stuff earmarked for burning around to the north side of the prison, where we had a large bonfire.

Meanwhile, the decision to demolish the prison had been announced, and had aroused some public comment from a few indi-viduals wishing to have it preserved. In the local historical interest, an agreement was reached with the Berlin Senate Chancellery for me to escort representatives from the *Landesbildstelle* (city photographic records) and the *Landeskonservator* (city conservation office) on a tour of the cleared prison, with the exception of the Allied Cell Block, with a military photographer to take pictures of those aspects of the prison architecture they wished to keep a record of. It was further agreed with the Senate Chancellery that these pictures would not be released or put on public display without the prior consent of the Allies.

The Governing Mayor was anxious to avoid a lobby building up on the demolition issue, so it was decided that the Royal Engineers would make a demonstrative start to the overall task. To make it look as if civilian contractors were at work, they were issued with blue overalls and safety hats in different colours. This proved to be a bit of a farce, however, for they were using military vehicles and equipment, and of course they marched to and from work in formation along the interior road from their barracks next door. Their first move was to take down some of the courtyard wall so that debris thrown down into the yard could be periodically swept aside by a bulldozer. First to go were the chapel windows, and soon afterwards the pews and organ pipes were being hurled through to smash on the cobbles below. Across the street a bevy of photographers recorded the message.

The Governors had given approval for the Sappers to go in on condition that a military guard be mounted on Hess's Portakabin, since clearance for its destruction had yet to be given. (This turned out to be dependent upon the production of Professor Cameron's full autopsy report.) It was arranged that the guard from one of the infantry battalions would provide a sentry while the Royal Engineers were working within the prison, but the very next morning after the operation began Darold and Chernykh went round to check and not only found that there was no sentry, but caught two Royal Engineers about to demolish it!

Adding insult to injury, the newspapers that day contained pictures of the Sappers working on the roof of the Administration Block, some of whom were taking photographs of each other. Consequently I had to face quite a barrage from my colleagues when I arrived a little later for our regular weekly meeting. I promptly telephoned the Chief of Staff with our grievances and matters were rapidly put to rights. It was said that all the films and cameras were confiscated, but I doubt if this was achieved. From that point on the Portakabin was sealed off with barbed wire and guarded by two armed Royal Engineer sentries.

On the afternoon of 1 September, as Chairman Governor, I gave a farewell party for all the employees. They displayed a surprising camaraderie, despite the variety of nationalities and educational backgrounds. Even Mr Whittacker, one of the original British warders from the old colonial prison service and by then in his eighties, turned up for the event.

Once established in House No. 24, it was decided that the first task was to prepare items belonging to Hess for return to the family. The gramophone records had been inadvertently destroyed during the move and, as related earlier, the personal items had been stolen from the Governors' safe, but we still had to consider the masses of photographs, books and correspondence remaining. Hess's catholic library had been moved from the Cell Block into the American flag room, so Darold and his two remaining warders settled down to checking the books for prison stamps and entries in the prisoner's handwriting.

Chernykh produced some chemicals for eliminating the inked impressions made by the prison stamps from the back of the mass of photographs sent him by the family that Hess had accumulated over the years. It was a messy job, involving several applications with the aid of cotton wool, and the fumes were such that the warders could only spend half an hour at a time before being forced to take a break, even when working with the help of surgical masks. When the first batch of chemicals ran out, the British Chief Warder undertook to get fresh supplies from the BMH. The formula he took with him turned out to be the same as for a domestic toilet cleaner, which proved to be far more effective and less unpleasant to work with. About 2,000 photographs were treated in this way, and with the hundreds of books of Hess's library and his letters, they amounted to a consignment of fifteen boxes that were eventually despatched to Andrea Hess at the end of September.

Eventually the Four Powers agreed that the SIB investigation had covered all the points required, and on 18 September we finally received permission to destroy the Portakabin. I immediately convened a meeting of the Governors to authorise our next steps, after which we all trooped out to watch one of the Royal Engineers fasten the Portakabin to his bulldozer with a steel cable and then drag it out to the bonfire site, where it was thumped and crushed by the machine until unrecognisable. Petrol was poured over it and set alight. Once the fire was going I threw into it the electric cable and Hess's clothing and walking-stick that had been held as evidence by the SIB, and which I had signed for that morning. By 12.30pm the destruction was complete and we trooped out of the prison for the last time, officially handing over the prison site to the British military.

A week later Andrea Hess and Dr Seidl came to see me to collect the suicide note. BMG wanted me also to give them the copy of the autopsy report reserved for the family, but I was unable to do this as the Board had objected that the report had yet to be seen by their own Medical Advisers, and they did not think it correct that the Hess family should receive a copy ahead of them.

Andrea Hess and Seidl came to my office at the British Sector Headquarters compound, close to the Olympic Stadium. It was an extremely awkward meeting for me, primarily because I was not authorised to reveal that certain items of Hess's personal property, due to be returned to the family, had been stolen from the prison. I did not know whether they were aware of the thefts, as reported in Clive Freeman's *Sunday Times* article, nor did I know at the time that they

had an unauthorised copy of the Governors' Recommendations list-
ing the items that should be returned to the family.

Frau Hess looked and acted a little strained, as well she might,
for she had had to handle everything herself since her husband's
heart attack after the second autopsy, including the secret burial. I
admired her courage, but there was still a certain underlying antipa-
thy between us. Also, with the family lawyer present, I had to be
very careful of what I said.

I started by handing her both sheets of the letter she had written
to the prisoner, on the back of one of which was the suicide note. In
answer to my query she confirmed that it bore her signature. I then
informed her that I proposed sending on to her the autopsy report
as soon as it had been cleared by the Medical Advisers. She nodded,
and then asked what had happened to the organs that had been
found to be missing from the body at the second autopsy. I told her
that they had been taken to the United Kingdom by Dr Cameron
for detailed examination to ensure that there were no foreign toxic
elements present that might have been responsible for the death.
I said that this laboratory process took several weeks to complete,
hence the delay in producing the final report.

Frau Hess then asked why there had been such conflicting – and
delayed – press statements about the death. I explained briefly what
had happened, about the need for Four Power agreement to a statement covering a circumstance – suicide – that had not been catered
for in the contingency planning. When she tried to pursue this
further, Dr Seidl intervened to say that the behaviour of the Four
Powers was understandable.

I then informed them that the preparation of items for return
to the family was now almost complete, and that we proposed
despatching the consignment of cartons of books, magazines, photographs and letters by parcel service to her home address, if she
agreed. In answer to their questions about the gramophone records
and personal effects, and despite the fact that news of thefts from the

14. Tower No. 3 seen from the prisoner's excercise path with evidence of the previous Allied prisoners' work showing under the trees on the right.

15. The guards' track leading into the broader prisoner's path in the north-western corner of the garden, with the Portakabin beyond.

16. Christmas in the Governors' Mess 1985, with Michel Planet, 'Katya', Tony Le Tissier, Lt Col Chernykh flanked by two BRIXMIS interpreters, Darold Keane and Senior Lieutenant Dimitri Naumenko.

17. Explosion in the Governors' Mess, 23 October 1986; the wrecked dining room.

18. The Portakabin in the garden.

19. The state of the Portakabin following the evacuation.

20. The suicide cable in place with the secure knot to the window handle.

21. The slip knot (in line with the top of the skirting board) and abandoned medical kit.

22. Inside the Cell block after clearance – The view from the entrance with the Medical Orderly's Room on the left and the Duty Chief Warder's Office on the right.

23. Inside the Cell Block after clearance – The view from the prisoner's end with all the cell doors open.

24. Inside the Cell Block after clearance – The prisoner's main cell and the entrance to the spiral staircase.

25. Inside the Cell Block after clearance – The prisoner's television room, outside which the Duty Warder would normally be stationed.

26. Soldiers of the 1st Battalion, The King's Own Scottish borderers, here seen in Towers Nos. 4 and 5, continued to guard the empty prison until demolition.

27. The clearance bonfire site where the Portakabin and other items associated with Hess were later destroyed.

28. & 29. The prison site completely cleared, except for trees.

30. The temporary Mess in No. 24 where the run-down of the prison administration was completed after the Royal Engineers had surrounded the building with Dannert wire on Soviet request. Nos. 25, 25A and Smuts Barracks in the background. The low wall on the right once carried and electrified fence.

31. Aerial view of the Britannia Centre in 1991. The two trees growing out of the patio are the horse chestnuts of the old prison courtyard. The clusters of trees to the rear are relics of Hess' garden.

prison had appeared in the press some time previously, I stuck, albeit somewhat red-faced, to the line that all the remaining items had been destroyed by decision of the Four Powers. When Dr Seidl protested that the leather flying-suit had been borrowed for the flight and did not belong to Hess, I told him, quite truthfully, that it too had been burnt.

They then asked about Dr Seidl's previous request to see the Portakabin and the extension cable. By what authority he imagined he would have been allowed to investigate the matter himself was beyond me but, to his obvious concern, I told them that the Portakabin had been destroyed and the cable burnt with it. Escorting them on their way out from the building once our meeting was over, I took the opportunity of asking Frau Hess how her husband was getting on. She told me that he was making a good recovery, but would be another five weeks in the convalescent home.

Meanwhile the task of clearing up at the prison continued. I had found a Berlin firm specialising in photocopying and microfilming from whom we could hire the necessary equipment for producing copies of the prison records for all Four Powers. As our financial representative, Michel Planet approached his contact in the *Senator für Justiz* Department and informed him of our intentions and the estimated cost, information that was received gratefully, as the department had not known what to expect. At this stage we reckoned to be finished roughly at the end of January, all being well, but we could not guarantee this because of the uncertainty of the factors involved.

The next stage was to set the remaining warders to preparing the archives for microfilming under the direct supervision of the Governors. Some of the files required re-sorting into more logical arrangements, particularly the older ones covering the early days of the administration.

The FCO Library and Records Department in London were particularly sceptical about our microfilming project, apparently as a result of their own experience with the old India Office records. They queried, among other things, the ability of our team of amateurs to get each document in turn correctly in focus, but in fact the equipment offered to us must have been technically far more advanced than that previously used in London. All the focusing was fully automatic, and minor problems in setting up the apparatus properly were soon resolved.

Each film could take 2,500 sheets of paper, so we divided the material into blocks of 500 sides for copying, and eventually ended up with enough material for thirty-six films. Chernykh quite rightly insisted upon waiting until this stage of preparation was complete before going on to the actual microfilming. On 22 October, Michel and Chernykh, with Dmitri Naumenko and 'Katya' (the American interpreter), went to spend a day at the firm that had hired us the equipment, in order to study the techniques used, and returned confident that they could handle it. The basic equipment consisted of a filming unit containing two cameras, thus automatically producing two copies of the filmed material. This was operated almost entirely by Chernykh, who changed from his uniform into jeans and sweater to do so, and was assisted by Katya, although Michel also operated the machine a few times. A darkroom was improvised to enable Chernykh to load the film into the magazines, the most complicated part of the operation. One set of films was completed each morning and the following day taken by two warders to the firm for processing. It was then checked on a reader in the afternoon and, if satisfactory, taken back for further copying the next day.

It was eventually decided to produce eight identical copies in all, two for each nation, one for the capitals and one for local reference, as it was thought that if any queries arose they would most likely be addressed to the Berlin end of the service concerned. Apart from one or two initial problems remedied by fine adjustments to the machine, the quality proved extraordinarily good.

Once the microfilming operation was complete, the original documents were burnt in a bonfire behind the building under the supervision of the Governors.

Meanwhile, civilian demolition contractors had moved in on the old prison site, knocking a large gap in the perimeter wall then erecting their own security fences and gate within the military compound. All the mature trees were bound with corsets of upright baulks of timber to protect them, and soon a whole lot of what looked like brand-new equipment moved in and the demolition began. First the upper stories were smashed in with a ball swung from a crane, then excavators climbed over the heaps of rubble and loaded the seemingly endless 'conveyor belt' of massive trucks and trailers, which then took their loads down Wilhelmstrasse to fill a disused sandpit on the Gatow ranges. Rumours circulated that individual bricks were being sold as souvenirs at phenomenal prices, but in reality there are so many buildings in Berlin of the same era, and built of similar bricks baked to Prussian standards, that such 'souvenirs' could be produced from anywhere. However, a policeman escorting one of the trucks was observed taking a brick from the sandpit area and was subsequently severely disciplined.

Of course, a tremendous amount of dust and noise accompanied this operation, and once the in-filling of the soil began, this being mainly loose sand, there were also massive vibrations transmitted to the buildings around from the hard-packing machines, making life in House No. 24 extremely difficult.

By the beginning of December, Chernykh could confidently forecast the photography of the documents being finished by 10 January 1988. The problem then arose as to how to set about the final stages. As the minutes of the final meeting had to be included on the microfilm, we would have to organise matters in such a way as to declare ourselves dissolved at a fixed time a few days after that last meeting.

After lunch following our brief weekly meeting on 23 December, we had the customary exchange of gifts before breaking up for the holiday period. Monday the 28th was a British holiday, although the others turned up for work. Next day Chernykh produced a schedule for the final period, and this was accepted by the Board. The last meeting would be on 6 January, the building handed over to the British authorities on the 14th, and the remaining staff dismissed after duty on the 15th, when our administration would be dissolved at 4pm. (His proposal as it was accepted actually stated 12–2pm, but this was later changed.)

I suddenly realised that I had precious little time in which to arrange for military help with the disposal of the keys and the prison seal, for British troops were off duty until Monday, 4 January. However, the Ordnance Services turned up trumps when contacted, and within twenty-four hours two warders were off in a BMG minibus with the steel box of keys, cell door labels and the prison seal, for dumping, unopened, by crane into a smelting furnace at Tegel in their presence.

The other problem that needed solving urgently was that of the architectural drawings we had discovered during the clear-out of the first floor of the Administration Block. I had brought the subject up at our Governors' meeting on 4 December 1987, saying that I thought they had artistic and historical merit, and that once all those drawings concerning the modernisation of the prison or its use by the Allies had been destroyed, those of the external buildings should be handed to the PSA to assist them with their restoration (these buildings were to be incorporated into the proposed British garrison welfare and NAAFI shopping centre to be built on the prison site), and the others in due course handed to the appropriate Berlin authorities for conservation. Although Planet and Keane readily agreed, Chernykh immediately opposed the idea, saying that he saw no merit in it. His arguments were such that I realised that if I was to achieve anything I would have to get the British Political Adviser to speak to his counterpart at the Soviet Embassy. The Political Adviser was not prepared to bring this up as a prime subject but, with time pressing, he finally telephoned his counterpart and, about a week later, back came the proposal that, should some expert agree that the drawings were worth preserving, then they should be microfilmed so that each nation would receive a full set, and the originals should then be divided up among the four nations for retention.

Now, with time so short, it was decided that the only non-German 'expert' BMG could call upon was the head of the British Council in Berlin, who was *ipso facto* also 'cultural adviser' to BMG. On the morning of the day of our penultimate meeting, our 'expert' was ill in bed, so it was his deputy, a woman, whom I invited along to inspect my treasures. She, having made the proviso that her opinion should not be quoted as being that of the British Council, arrived promptly and immediately expressed enthusiasm over the nature and quality of the drawings. Chernykh acted as if he had expected this, but it was now up to me to arrange for the drawings to be microfilmed, so the same afternoon I went along to see the head of the firm we had been dealing with. He deployed his usual whirlwind style, and within ten minutes I had seen the equipment and met the operator, who said that he could do the job from 10am onwards next day.

By about 1pm that day Katya was back with four sets of 88mm microfiche, of which each shot had been separately focused by the operator. 'Katya' handed out the sets before we sat down to lunch.

January had brought me back into the Chair, so I had arranged to hold a penultimate meeting of the Board on Tuesday the 5th, at which we would conclude outstanding business on the agenda and approve the text of our final meeting on the following day. At this penultimate meeting the arrangements for the copying and distribution of the architectural drawings were approved. Michel declared the financial affairs to be in order, and Chernykh confirmed that notice of dismissal had been issued to the remaining staff. It was agreed that we should make out a certificate covering the destruction of the original archives when that had been completed on the

11th, and the microfilming equipment would be returned on the 8th. The British draft of the text of the final meeting was accepted quite readily. Consequently our last meeting, the 2,102nd, lasted only a few minutes.

With the agreement of the others, I pasted copies of the minutes of that last meeting on the back of four drawings of the Main Gate that I had had framed, and we passed them round the table for each other to sign. Then we each took one as a souvenir before retiring to the bar for a glass of champagne.

On Monday, 11 January, the next working day, I set to sorting the drawings into categories divisible by four. Somehow they worked out reasonably well into twenty original drawings dated 1 September 1877, twelve subsequent drawings, eight drawings of particular artistic merit, four of the gatehouse, four of the workshops, four designs for the isolation exercise area, and the remainder drawings of specific details. I then improvised a lottery among ourselves for their division between the four nations. A few days later Michel said that I could take his drawings, which he had left on top of a cabinet in his flag room. Chernykh saw me doing this, but made no comment. The following day Darold rang and told me that he was sending the American copies back to the prison for me to collect, which I did.

In view of the mutual agreement to retain these drawings, it was decided that they could only be handed to the *Landesarchiv* (city archives) as a permanent loan under conditions that drew no public attention to the act, and with a ban on putting them on public display without Allied consent. This was in fact part of the agreement with the Senate Chancellery, previously mentioned, for making a photographic record of the prison. Arrangements were made for the *Landesbildstelle* to make copies of the microfiche of the full set of drawings for themselves, for the *Landesarchiv*, and for the *Landeskonservator*.

As we had approached Christmas, the time came when we had to consider how we should conclude the operation. The French and Americans were totally opposed to holding a farewell party at the prison, but both the British and American Commandants were keen that the occasion should be suitably marked. Certain difficulties arose about the participation of the Commandants, whose attendance could have been misinterpreted by the media, so I offered to hold the event at my home as a lunchtime reception for all the Governors, Medical and Legal Advisers, and interpreters who had been involved. The British Commandant kindly sponsored the affair, even though he himself could not attend.

I had had the Berlin Police warned beforehand, and so they had three or four men keeping an eye on things when the guests arrived at noon on Friday 15 January 1988. There were three soldiers' wives from the waitresses' pool taking coats, serving drinks and washing up, and a cook sergeant from the Headquarters Mess, all working under the supervision of a warrant officer catering adviser, who had arranged a particularly good curry menu with a chicken fricassee alternative. My wife had arranged our reception rooms so that there were places for everyone to sit and eat in small groups.

Colonel Perevertsev, the Soviet Inspecting Officer from SERB, led the Potsdam team, Dr Jashin and his deputy represented the Soviet Embassy, and we also had a full complement of Governors, Legal Advisers, Medical Advisers and interpreters from the Western Allies.

Champagne was served when the time came for serving the sweet, giving me the opportunity to say a few brief words thanking everyone for their co-operation in the administration of the prison. Unfortunately, however, I had stipulated '1200–1400 hrs' on my invitations, so promptly at 2pm the Soviet colonel marched his officers out, to run the gauntlet of two television cameras that had meanwhile been set up. They were shortly followed by the other guests and within minutes the house was clear.

Some articles in the newspapers next day reported a 'Champagne Breakfast', but to me the most amusing, and one that aroused many ribald comments from members of my family and others, was Catherine Field's in the *Observer* of 17 January 1988, which began:

> Last Friday, four men and their companions sat down in a pala-tial West Berlin home to enjoy a noble banquet, with wines of the best vintage, excellent brandy and the sort of service suitable for an occasion of stately importance.
>
> The lunch has been a regular monthly gathering for more than 40 years, with each of the four men taking it in turn to host the occasion. And although the faces have changed over the decades, the format has not.
>
> But this meal was the last – a final meal to bid farewell to an era of East-West co-operation which, throughout the Cold War, was a unique and valuable contact between the Western Allies and the Soviet Union.
>
> The four men at table last Friday – Anthony Le Tissier, from Britain, Michel Planet, from France, Darold 'Danny' Keane, from the US, and Lt Col Tschernick, from the Soviet Union – were marking their last day as governors of Spandau War Crimes Prison.

So it was all over. Or was it?

# XII

# Aftermath

A series of events dating from early 1988 onwards and concerning Rudolf Hess gave the growing impression of 'he's dead but he won't lie down'!

Firstly there was the publication in March 1988 of Dr Hugh Thomas's second book, *A Tale of Two Murders*, with all its attendant publicity. Then came news that the Director of Public Prosecutions had tasked Scotland Yard with an investigation into murder by persons unknown as a result of Thomas's allegations, which had been followed by a programme in the BBC2 television *Newsnight* series on 28 February 1989.

However, what got me thinking seriously about doing something positive to counter the allegations of murder or false identity, and all the time-wasting caused by the mischief and myths that were being created, was when the British Military Government suddenly decided that I should give an unattributable interview to the Bonn correspondent of the *Financial Times*, David Marsh. He, however, then promptly became involved in the events on the Austrian-Hungarian border and the unleashing of the flood of East German refugees to the Federal Republic, and so had to put aside the topic for a while. Then, barely a week later, Bernard Levin produced another scathing article in *The Times* about Wolf-Rüdiger Hess's attitude towards his father, apparently triggered off by the news that Wolf-Rüdiger was about to release a new book on the second anniversary of his father's death. Thinking it over, it occurred to me that both Mr Marsh and Mr Levin were really preaching to the converted when one considered the readership of their respective newspapers. I therefore decided to try to put the record straight in the public mind by writing an account of my own experiences in this matter, in the hope that the FCO would permit its release for publication.

Dr Thomas's second book, *A Tale of Two Murders*, extended the ridiculous theme of his earlier work that Prisoner No. 7 had not been the true Rudolf Hess; it also gave a highly imaginative description of the circumstances of the prisoner's death in which gaps in factual knowledge were liberally plastered over with pure invention.

Colonel Hamer-Philip of the BMH assisted me in the production of a ten-page paper comparing the numerous errors in the new areas of Thomas's book with the facts known to us. For instance, Dr Thomas claimed that the prisoner had never suffered bronchial attacks, whereas his medical records showed a history of respiratory problems occurring in winter, and that a bad chest infection in the winter of 1986/87 had necessitated his hospitalisation. He also claimed that the prisoner only picked at his food, whereas, despite his fastidiousness about the substance of his diet, the enormous quantities Hess habitually consumed were quite remarkable for a person of his age.

Not having ever entered the prison, Dr Thomas's description of the 'shed' in the garden, with its floor covered in dust, wood-shavings and metal-filings, bears no resemblance to Hess's Portakabin. The dramatic inclusion of several coils of yellow electrical flex, left behind by a German firm repairing the 4,000-volt killer-wire, is quite awe-inspiring, the electrified fence that had once surrounded the prison walls having vanished long before I ever saw the place. And contrary to Dr Thomas's assertion that a German firm would have been used for such a wiring job, when the wiring of the security lighting system had previously required replacement, the German contractors' estimates had proved so exorbitant that British troops had been called in to do the job.

It would be tedious to go through all the many errors that occurred in Dr Thomas's description of events on the afternoon of Hess's death, but suffice it to say that I would love to have seen the corkscrew-shaped stretcher needed to get Hess up the spiral staircase! The description of the Governor's meeting on the evening of 17 August 1987, the day that Hess died, is so at variance with the facts that it is best ignored. But then, so is Dr Thomas's whole book, for that matter.

Another book published in 1988, Wulf Schwarzwäller's *Rudolf Hess – The Deputy*, which appeared in both English and German versions, ended by alleging that, in accordance with the instructions of the Four Powers, Hess's remains had been secretly cremated and then scattered over the sea from an aircraft!

On 10 December 1988, a former British warder at Spandau Allied Prison, Steven Timson, and his brother-in-law, Paul Warman, were arrested in the Crest Hotel, Hamburg, while attempting to blackmail Wolf-Rüdiger Hess for DM 500,000 for the return of his father's stolen property. Timson claimed that he had found the items in a bag while cleaning out the prison after the death of the prisoner, thus implying that someone else had actually removed the items earlier from the clothing store in the Cell Block and from the Governors' safe. However, among the items recovered were several documents that could only have been taken from the archives at the time that some of the warders, including Timson, were helping to sort them out in House No. 24 prior to microfilming, this being after the complete clearance of the prison and the only time he or any other warder could have had access to such documents. In my opinion this was clear evidence of systematic theft by Timson, Paul Warman being merely an accessory after the fact.

Although I was asked to call on the prosecutor beforehand, and did so, making a statement establishing these circumstances, it seems that the Berlin court was anxious to dispose of the case with the minimum fuss. The accused's pleas of 'guilty' to attempted black-mail were accepted, and they were awarded suspended sentences which removed them quickly from the scene. Re-examination of the SIB file showed that Timson had been Duty Chief Warder on the evening of 19 August 1986, when he would have had the opportunity of fishing the keys out of the wall safe and thereby getting access to the clothing and other items of personal property.

On 28 February 1989, the BBC2 *Newsnight* programme devoted itself to presenting the allegations made by Dr Hugh Thomas and Wolf-Rüdiger Hess concerning the death of the prisoner. A bomb-shell witness was Melaouhi, the Medical Orderly.

In this programme, Melaouhi made statements and allegations on the following lines:

a. When Melaouhi arrived at the Portakabin, Hess's body was some distance away from the window where it is claimed he had hanged himself, the furniture was thrown about as if a wrestling match had taken place, and it looked as if someone had tried to kill him and he had tried to save himself.

b. Melaouhi had been summoned from his lunch in the canteen.

c. It took him about fifteen minutes to gain admittance through the Main Gate.

d. His way to the Cell Block where he kept his kit was blocked, and he had to persuade a soldier to let him through into the garden area. It should have taken him four minutes to get to the prisoner but on this occasion it took forty.

e. He saw no cable round the prisoner's neck, but the extension cable was still in place, one end connected to the lamp and one to the wall socket.

f. There were three people present, the warder, whom he knew, and two men in US Army uniforms who should not have been there.

g. Hess was so weak in his last months that he needed a special chair to help him stand up. He walked, bent, with a cane, and was almost blind. His hands were crippled with arthritis. He could not tie his own shoelaces, let alone lift his hands high enough to kill himself.

h. He must have been murdered.

I was simply astounded by Melaouhi's presentation. When the SIB had tried to obtain a witness statement from him during the course of their investigation, he had refused to co-operate, appealing to me in an almost hysterical manner to be excused, and saying that he was just a nurse and wanted nothing to do with the police. This had happened on three separate occasions as the SIB vainly tried to obtain a statement from him. Having known Melaouhi well for a long time before this, and knowing his calm, gentle nature and the respect with which he was held by everyone, including the Medical Advisers, I found this attitude at the time of Hess's death and the SIB investigation completely out of character, utterly inexplicable.

Having seen the *Newsnight* programme I concluded that the ideas now being expressed had either entered, or been fed, into Melaouhi's mind before the SIB approach, and that he must have thought that he was being asked to co-operate in the cover-up of a crime committed under state auspices!

Melaouhi claimed that he had been summoned by telephone from his lunch in the canteen in House No. 24. However, the French Duty Chief Warder reported to his Governor that he had tried unsuccessfully for over twenty minutes to contact Melaouhi at his apartment, at the Mess, and within the prison, which would indicate that Melaouhi only received the message that he was wanted when he eventually appeared at the Mess. In other words, his absence over this period from the areas in which he was expected to be found substantially contributed to his delayed arrival at the Portakabin.

Some further delay in gaining admittance can be explained by the British Main Gate Warder being on the telephone carrying out his 'Paradox' tasks by summoning the Governors. He was the only one with a key, so the guard could not help. The Main Gate Warder stated that he shouted after Melaouhi that he would probably not be able to get to the garden through the prison building, and asked the guard to let him through one of the side gates. The Duty Chief Warder was in fact in the garden at the time, and says that he saw the cable still hanging at the window of the Portakabin. Variations in the timings quoted in the witness statements make a precise analysis impossible, but the first American combat medic says that he checked his watch, which showed 2.40pm when he was summoned by radio. The medic found the gates held open for him and ran straight through to the Portakabin, where he says Melaouhi arrived shortly afterwards, although the guard sergeant says that Melaouhi was already there when he arrived with the first medic. The gate log showed Melaouhi booked in at 2.45pm. Despite the lack of precision, there can be little doubt that Melaouhi's claim of imposed lengthy delays on route is entirely without foundation.

The state of the Portakabin is easily explained by Jordan's actions in freeing and trying to resuscitate Hess, and those of the others called to the scene. The furniture was light and easily flung aside. The cable had already been removed by Jordan from the prisoner's neck. There was more than one standard lamp there, so there would have been more than one cable.

The presence of the men in US Army uniform is self-evident. Both Jordan's appeal for assistance with first aid and one by the Main Gate Warder to the guard had resulted in two medics appearing where normally they would have had no business to be. Melaouhi did not know them and had no cause to, either professionally or socially, but the American soldiers all knew each other as members of the same unit, and any military outsiders would have been noticed. Melaouhi omitted to say that the medics worked with him to try and resuscitate the prisoner. Yet these allegations were to lead to speculation that Hess's death was all part of a British plot carried out by members of the Special Air Service Regiment disguised as American soldiers!

Finally, Melaouhi's description of Hess's medical condition conflicts both with the medical facts and the observations of other people who knew him. 'Hess was so weak' – yet Melaouhi supervised his efforts on an exercise bicycle every morning. 'He was bent and walked with a cane' – agreed, but he was not 'almost blind,' as I have described elsewhere. Hess was 'crippled with arthritis. He could not tie his shoelaces, let alone lift his hands high enough to kill himself.' He wore a truss because of hernia problems, and probably found bending over to tie his shoelaces difficult, but he had Melaouhi to help him in such matters. Nevertheless, his fingers were still nimble enough to write legibly and carry out other tasks, such as tying a simple slip knot in an extension cable.

Whatever may have been Melaouhi's motives for making these allegations and distortions of the facts, it has been suggested that he must have been 'got at' by interested parties at quite an early stage. From enjoying a salary at the prison that was well above average, because of the need to be constantly on call, he then had a hard time finding new employment, despite the high recommendations he received from all three Western Allies. Their own regulations unfortunately prevented them from employing non-German local staff in their hospitals, and he came up against the usual German prejudice against foreigners when applying for work in the civil hospitals in Berlin, despite his all-German medical training, qualifications and experience. Eventually all he was able to obtain was a night job at a hospital at the end of the city furthest from where he lived.

On the same *Newsnight* programme, Professor Spann, the German pathologist who had carried out the second autopsy, explained that none of the normal evidence of hanging was evident. This statement, however, was based entirely on the assumption that if Hess had committed suicide by hanging, then it presumed a hangman's knot and suspension from a certain height, neither of which applied in this case, as I have previously explained. Two black-and-white drawings used to illustrate the points, firstly of the hanging showing a person fully suspended by a normal hangman's knot, and then of Jordan and two men in US Army uniform standing around in the Portakabin just looking at the body on the floor, only served to emphasise the misconceptions contained in this television programme.

Also in this programme, and repeated in the book he released in August 1989, Wolf-Rüdiger alleged that the suicide note must have been forged, because, among other things, there was no reference to the grandchildren of whom Hess was extremely fond, and the form of signature was one that he had not used for several years. Yet Hess's mind may well have been focused on other matters, including 'Freiburg'. When planning to take his own life, he must surely have been thinking more of his own past than about the grandchildren he had never seen except on film or in photographs.

Although he had not operated under laboratory conditions, the handwriting expert we had called in had come to the conclusion that the handwriting on the note was consistent with Hess's writing style, and that it had been written with one of the assortment of pens found in Hess's pockets, another of these pens having been used by him to mark Andrea's letter on the other side of the paper.

Wolf-Rüdiger also alleged that the Soviets had been about to agree to the release of his father. He based this belief on the outcome of his meeting with Mr Grinin, the Political Adviser at the Soviet Embassy, coupled with the imminence of the visit of President von Weizsäcker of the German Federal Republic to Moscow. Yet none of the Western Allies had perceived any intimation that this was even likely. On the contrary, the latest communications had indicated that First Secretary Gorbachev would be unwilling to go against the public feeling of the mass of the Soviet people, to whom Rudolf Hess remained the living symbol of the Nazi era. Nor does Wolf-Rüdiger's written account of his meeting with Mr Grinin match his own interpretation that it had given cause for hope of release.

Then, on 1 April 1989, *Figaro* magazine published an article by Jean-Pax Méfret entitled '*Document Rudolf Hess – les nouvelles raisons qui font douter de son suicide*', which, backed with copies of prison documents and statements from unnamed persons, cast further doubts on the official version of Hess's death.

Finally, however, in August 1989, the Crown Prosecution Service wrote to the Metropolitan Police to say that they considered that there was insufficient evidence to justify further enquiries. (The SIB inquiry had been conducted in accordance with normal English police procedures and had only closed, and the exhibits in the case had been destroyed, when all Four Powers had given approval.) The case was thus considered closed for good, except in the unlikely event that some credible evidence should come to light. Dr Hugh Thomas was also apparently informed on these lines.

Not long after starting to put some notes together about Hess and Spandau, I recalled that there had been mention in the German newspapers of Wolf-Rüdiger announcing the release of a new book on the occasion of the second anniversary of his father's death. With a little difficulty I managed to obtain a copy of his *Mord an Rudolf Hess?*, which had been produced by an obscure publisher outside Munich. The book turned out to be a highly emotional presentation of Wolf-Rüdiger's views on what had occurred. Included in it was a translation into German of the *Figaro* article, the two autopsy reports, and another translation into German of the Governors' Recommendations of 29 June 1983 concerning the procedures for the termination of the prison administration following the death of Hess. Not only were the British the villains in this drama, Churchill and Thatcher being the arch-villains, of course, but Anthony Le Tissier (at least I was in august company) held the centre of the stage. The representatives of the other nations were depicted as being impotent in the face of the machinations of Perfidious Albion. Professor Spann had appeared at the press conference launching this book, seemingly in support of the murder claim. So the mischief continued.

The sad thing about *Mord an Rudolf Hess?* was the state of mind it revealed. As Bernard Levin wrote so aptly in *The Times* of 4 September 1989, in his article 'Sins of the father that can never be erased':

> That, then, is the man who now accuses the British Government of murdering his father and who demands that we should admire that father without reserve. I do not of course repine at my championing of the cause of Hess senior's release because I thought it right, despite the character of the prisoner; the character of the prisoner's son was irrelevant to my pleas. But now that argument has been laid to rest with the martyred Deputy Führer's body, I fervently hope that we shall never hear from Hess junior again, whether on the subject of the sinister Jews or the British murder of his father or anything else. If we do, I shall remind him that he still has not spoken a word of criticism of his father or his father's career, despite the fact that the war criminal's last words from the Nuremberg dock were:
>
> > I am not defending myself against the accusers, whose right to bring charges against me and my fellow Germans I deny. I do not argue against accusations concerned with events which are domestic German matters, and therefore nothing to do with foreigners. I raise no objection to statements aimed at attacking my honour or that of the entire German people. I consider such offensive remarks by adversaries as compliments. I had the privilege of acting for many years of my life under the greatest son my country has produced in its thousand-year history.

As the proverb has it: the apple doesn't fall far from the tree.

Then, on 17 December 1989, just when one would have thought that events in eastern Europe and the collapse of the Berlin Wall would have let this matter slip into oblivion, the prestigious American television news programme, *Sixty Minutes*, revived the allegations of a British cover-up with its ace reporter Ed Bradley interviewing Eugene Bird, Wolf-Rüdiger, Melaouhi, and Professor Spann.

The American Medical Adviser responded by writing to the producer of that programme on 8 January 1990 (spelling as per original):

> As the physician who, along with the British Hospital Commander, pronounced Rudolph Hess dead, I found your recent report on his death inaccurate and misleading. His medical condition certainly would have permitted him to knot an extension cord and commit suicide. Furthermore, other parts of your story directly contradict descriptions from the first U.S. medics to arrive at the scene after the suicide and what I observed during the post mortum examination of Hess's remains. From August 1986 to August 1987, I saw, spoke with and examined Rudolph Hess frequently. In my opinion, he was clearly capable of planning and carrying out his own death.

This theme – that Hess was murdered – was apparently also continued by Howard Brenton in his play *Hess is Dead*, or *HID*, which was produced by the Royal Shakespeare Company at the Almeida Theatre in London, attracting comment in both the British and German press in early January 1990.

The *Sixty Minutes* programme had ignored Dr Hugh Thomas's allegations, but on 17 January 1990 Christopher Andrew devoted a complete BBC2 *Timewatch* programme to their investigation along the theme that official silences tend to encourage such conspiracy theories, which are then extremely difficult to disprove. Nevertheless, he was able to produce some most convincing evidence to achieve just this. Having tracked down Hess's original hospital records in the Bavarian Army archives in Munich, in which his lung-shot entry and exit wounds were repeatedly described as pea-sized, the expert opinion of Professor Bernard Knight, of the Department of Forensic Medicine at the University of Wales, was introduced to explain that normal fibrosing over the years would have reduced these scars to a size indistinguishable from those of a skin disease or made by scratching. Going on to Professor Spann's remarks about the straight, continuous bruise noted by him around Hess's neck, but not by Professor Cameron, Professor Knight commented to the effect that it was a well-known fact that such bruising became more evident with time after death. He also went on to say that Professor Spann's statement that, because the mark was horizontal it must be due to strangulation, was not true, in that there were some well known textbook cases to the contrary. Professor Knight then produced evidence of a similar case of hanging from a low suspension point, in which the same kind of marking had occurred.

This programme was widely commented on in the British press both before and after the event, and even gave rise to a long article in the Russian newspaper *Izvestia* on 27 January 1990.

The well-known historian Peter Padfield produced his book *Hess – The Führer's Disciple* in 1991. I had received a letter from him a year before asking for my co-operation, but had declined to reply, as I was working on my own account of what had occurred. It would therefore be unfair of me to comment adversely about his book now. However, it contains one interesting point I would like to refer to. Presumably resulting from an interview with Melaouhi, he writes that, on the morning of his death, Hess had asked Melaouhi to purchase a new kettle. This appears to be Melaouhi's excuse for not being available when the alarm was raised, but not one used by him at the time of the investigation. Hess's request would normally have been made by means of a *Gesuch* in writing to the Board of Governors, Melaouhi having no prison funds at his disposal for such purposes.

Although originally under a seventy-five-year secrecy ban, on 10 June 1992 the Public Record Office in London released about 1,100 papers covering Hess's flight to the United Kingdom and his detention and interrogations there. Only those documents containing the names of persons connected with the Secret Service, whose identities cannot be revealed, were withheld. In fact, these papers did little but confirm the fact that Hess's flight had been made without the knowledge or consent of his beloved Führer, Adolf Hitler.

Again, the television coverage was widespread, and included interviews with Dr Hugh Thomas, who happens to provide good subject material for the cameras, despite his cause. So the myths continue.

In (hopeful) conclusion, I would like to say that people will always believe what they want to believe. I do not, therefore, expect complete success in this attempt to lay the ghost, but at least I have tried to put the record straight for those who are willing to accept the truth as I know it and as I saw it.

In all, I believe that the Governors of Spandau Allied Prison, with the exception of Eugene Bird, conducted themselves humanely and conscientiously as representatives of their respective governments in the tending of the last of the major German war criminals in Allied hands. That Hess took his own life allowed him, in a way, the last laugh on us, for it was yet another unexpected event in the saga of that unique establishment.

# Glossary of abbreviations used in the text

ACA     Allied Control Authority
AK      Allied Kommandatura
APM    Assistant Provost-Marshal (Lieutenant-Colonel RMP)

BAOR  British Army of the Rhine
BASC   Berlin Air Safety Centre
BMG    British Military Government
BMH    British Military Hospital
BRIXMIS      British Commander-in-Chiefs' Mission to the Soviet Forces
           in Germany

CO      Commanding Officer
CSM    Company Sergeant-Major (Warrant Officer Second Class)

FCO     Foreign and Commonwealth Office

GDR    German Democratic Republic
GMFB  *Gouvernement Militaire Français de Berlin*
GRU    Soviet Military Intelligence
GSFG   Group of Soviet Forces in Germany

HQ      Headquarters

KGB    Soviet Ministry of State Security
*Kripo*   Berlin Criminal Police

NAAFI  Navy, Army and Air Force Institutes

PSA     Property Services Agency

QA      Quadripartite Agreement on Berlin of 1971

RAF     Royal Air Force
RE      Corps of Royal Engineers
RMP     Corps of Royal Military Police
RSM     Regimental Sergeant-Major (Warrant Officer First Class)

SERB    Soviet External Relations Branch (GSFG)
SIB     Special Investigations Branch (RMP)

Toc H   Talbot House – a welfare service providing canteen and newspaper
        facilities for the armed forces

# Index